A Permanent Becoming

A Permanent Becoming

A Contemporary Look at the Fruit of the Spirit

Alan Mann

Authentic

MILTON KEYNES ● COLORADO SPRINGS ● HYDERABAD

14 13 12 11 10 09 08   7 6 5 4 3 2 1

First published 2008 by Authentic Media
9 Holdom Avenue, Bletchley, Milton Keynes, Bucks, MK1 1QR, UK
1820 Jet Stream Drive, Colorado Springs, CO 80921, USA
OM Authentic Media, Medchal Road, Jeedimetla Village,
Secunderabad 500 055, A.P., India
www.authenticmedia.co.uk

Authentic Media is a division of IBS-STL U.K., limited by guarantee, with its
Registered Office at Kingstown Broadway, Carlisle, Cumbria CA3 0HA.
Registered in England & Wales No. 1216232. Registered charity 270162

British Library Cataloguing in Publication Data
A catalogue record for this book is available from the British Library

ISBN-13: 978-1-85078-783-9

Unless otherwise stated Scripture quotations are taken from the Contemporary
English Version (CEV) Copyright © 1995 by the Bible Society. Used by permission.

Cover Design by Fourninezero design.
Print Management by Adare
Printed and bound in Great Britain by J.H. Haynes & Co., Sparkford

For my daughter, Liberty

Where the Spirit of the Lord is, there is freedom.

2 Corinthians 3:17

Contents

Acknowledgements

Writing is a solitary endeavour, but it never takes place in a vacuum. Thanks, therefore, to Tim Dobson, Claire and Tim Lea, Pete and Lindsey Mansfield, Dave Mitchell, Mike Nicholson, Rachie Ross and Tim Summers, for the coffee, the lunches, the walks and the wisdom – much of which found its way into the book . . . *even if I've made it unrecognizable*.

Thanks to Steve Chalke MBE, who saw my potential and gave me my first writing job. I will forever be grateful, indebted and inspired . . . *and infamous!*

Thanks to Rob Parsons, Brian McLaren, David Oliver, Jason Clark and Chris Sunderland, who have supported and encouraged me (and my family), in so many ways.

Thanks also to Cheryl Wells, Bex Barker and Jane Hogg, who looked after my daughter Liberty, giving me the space to think, research and write . . . *and occasionally sleep.*

Last and first: Kay, I owe you everything, yet at times I feel like I give you so little. *Thank you for letting me pursue my dreams.*

A PERMANENT BECOMING / Zero
Under the Skin

```
┌─────────────────────────────────────────────────────┐
│                                                       │
│   Love              Joy                  Peace        │
│                                                       │
│        Patience                 Kindness              │
│                                                       │
│                 Goodness                              │
│                                                       │
│     Faithfulness              Gentleness              │
│                                                       │
│              Self-control                             │
│                                                       │
└─────────────────────────────────────────────────────┘
```

At first glance, the Fruit of the Spirit[1] appear extremely mundane. They are, after all, very ordinary, everyday words. Worse than ordinary, they're mostly 'nice' words. In adjective form, the kind of words you might use to describe your granny: 'Oh, she's really kind.' Or perhaps even the dog: 'Patch, what a faithful hound!'

Most of us would recognize the values they imply, but to coin a contemporary turn of phrase, 'They're not very sexy.'

After all, while we love our smoothies to be full of 'goodness', we'd rather be perceived as a bit more edgy: Do you have a wicked side? Not evil; just not goody-goody. An endearing sort of naughtiness that doesn't take life too seriously.

The truth is, most of us don't do mundane, do we? At least we don't aspire to the humdrum in life, even if the reality of our day-to-day existence is routine. We may well be a paper-pushing Mr or Ms Average, but inside we are Bond, Bono and Beckham; Madonna, Moss and M— (sorry, I couldn't think of another inspirational woman who fits with the alliteration, and I'm not prone to patience!).

It's not that we have anything particularly against the kind of virtues we see in the Fruit of the Spirit, nor against other people having them – after all, they're hardly going to make the world a bad place. Dull, yes. Bad, no. It's just that we don't seem to live in a culture that positively encourages faithfulness, patience, gentleness, kindness, goodness, self-control and the like. Neither our role models, nor our celebrities, nor advertisers, are minded to portray these things as desirable, or necessary for life, because we don't require them to.

A teacher I know retired after years of uncommonly faithful service at the same school. Though she had deeply enjoyed her time there, during her leaving speech she spoke this lament: 'Academic success is a right and proper pursuit for a school. But I would prefer it if we could have developed an ethos that favoured the pursuit of kindness. But sadly, that's not a government target.'

Single-mindedly we pursue what the world tells us counts as success, achievement and a fruitful and fulfilling use of our life.

Kindness? Well, at best, that's an extra-curricular activity.

In the world – and often just like it

Please don't get me wrong, I'm not a paragon of these virtues, tut-tutting at the world from my ivory church tower. Actually, truth be known, it was within the white-washed walls of the church that I began to feel this apathy towards the Fruit of the Spirit.

I seldom heard anyone talking about them. No one seemed to be wanting anyone to pray for them to be more gentle, good, loving, or joyful – myself included. As for being self-controlled? – heaven forbid!

Neither could I find much in print so that I could at least read about the Fruit of the Spirit – except that my local Christian bookshop did have rather a lot of Bibles, which mentions these virtues quite a lot.

Of course, what you can find lots of, both in print and in churches, is an interest in the *Gifts* of the Spirit: prophecy, speaking in tongues, words of knowledge, healing, and so on.

I guess Christians don't do mundane either – and on the surface, to our twenty-first-century sensibilities (and when compared to raising the dead), the Fruit of the Spirit can come across as a tad unexciting.

Yin and Yang

Let's be clear. I'm not suggesting that emphasizing the Gifts of the Spirit is a bad thing. After all, when I'm lying sick in a hospital bed, a bowl of *fruit* isn't much of a *gift*. But therein lies the issue. I'm seldom lying on my sick bed. What's more, I've had plenty of words of knowledge to keep me going for a few years yet. There's more than enough prophetic words in the Bible to discern without being offered more to weigh and wrestle with. And, as my old school reports make clear, I'm useless at 'foreign' languages.

Yet, on a day-to-day basis, I want people to be kind to me. Because of my foibles, friends and family have to find endless amounts of patience. I struggle with faithfulness in my relationships, both human and divine. I desire peace among the chaos that is modern life. I long to discover goodness in a world that seems to harbour so much anger and hatred. And I'd do anything to bring joy to my daughter.

The fact is, ordinarily, the Fruit of the Spirit is of supreme importance.

God wants all of us to have the Fruit in abundance, because of his desire for us to become like Jesus. On the other hand, no Christian has (or is intended to have) all the Gifts. Sadly, I know a great many people who feel that they are second-rate Christians because they don't appear to manifest any of the obvious Gifts. And yet the truth is, in God's eyes at least, they are all first rate, because, to a greater or lesser degree, the Fruit of the Spirit flows out of them, making them more like Christ.

But please don't mis-read me. I'm not seeking to promote a spiritual competition. It's not a case of either the Gifts or the Fruit of the Spirit. Rather, it should be a seeking after the Gifts and a desire to live Fruitful lives. For the Fruit without the Gifts lacks a certain dynamism. But be warned. Gifts that are exercised without the Fruit of the Spirit can be utterly destructive.

That said, by their nature, Gifts come and go. They may feel at the time like the pinnacle of spirituality, but in reality, they're ephemeral, fleeting, temporary. For everyone who prophesies will stop, and unknown languages will no longer be spoken.

But love never fails![2] Well, at least that's what Paul wrote!

Spiritual aspirations

Paradoxically, as many of the New Testament writers (and Jesus himself) suggest, it is the rather ordinary and human-sounding Fruit of the Spirit that makes us Christ-like – and to be Christ-like should be the central aspiration of the Christian life.

Actually, to be Christ-like should be the central aspiration of life – period. For to be Christ-like is to be what so many people long to be: authentic; fully awake, open to the world; self-aware; at one with ourselves, with others and the creation. To be at one with the Divine.

Isn't that what drives so much of our search for spirituality – the sense that there is more to life, more to me? That intuition that I have hidden depths, even if all my friends and work colleagues think I'm shallow.

Strange, then, that so little time is being given over to understanding and purposefully pursuing the Fruit of the Spirit. For what Jesus and others appear to be suggesting is that this is the spiritual framework, the matrix out of which we respond, act, live, develop, know and become known; that the Fruit of the Spirit leads us into that permanent becoming of who we are meant to be – human beings created in the image of God, as personified in the life of Jesus.

Peel

Given this apparent lack of interest in mundane spirituality, it might seem like literary suicide to write an entire book on the Fruit of the Spirit. Indeed, it might be a valid question to ask whether there is a book that can be written on the subject. After all, we know what it means to be good: help granny across the road and don't kick the cat. What else is there to know? Somehow, that doesn't feel like it's going to scratch our spiritual itch, or our yearning to connect more deeply with life as it's being lived in the third millennium.

But here lies our error: we only give the Fruit of the Spirit a surface reading, a cursory glance, because we assume that we understand their content and their call on our lives. They look ordinary, commonplace, lacking the complexities, energy and profundity that will generate within us spiritual depths. But if we think that, then we've not only missed their place, purpose and pervasiveness within the biblical narrative (and specifically in the life of Jesus), but we've failed to perceive their relevance to our contemporary context and the vitality they can bring to our spiritual formation as human beings.

The spiritual potency of the Fruit of the Spirit dwells in the interface between the narrative of Scripture and the story of our lives.

Therefore, what we really need to do is three-fold:

- We need to peel back the skin of the Fruit of the Spirit to discover the depths that lie underneath that unassuming exterior, letting Jesus, and the Spirit of God, define our understanding of love, joy, peace, patience, kindness, goodness, faithfulness, gentleness and self-control, not the culture we live in.

- We need to peel back the skin of the world we live in and so understand a little more deeply the stories we currently live by.

- We need to bring the two together so that we can give ourselves the chance to generate a genuine, meaningful, contemporary and life-changing Christian spirituality. Not just for our personal advantage, but for the sake of everyone who shares this world with us.

On the page

Philip Yancey says that he writes to discover. That he chooses a topic because he wants to learn, not because he knows. After all, what could be more tedious than committing to paper your certainties and the lucid thoughts in your head?

I'm with Philip on this one. A cliché it may be, but the following pages are intended to be part of an ongoing journey, that has no terminus this side of eternity. To that end, they are as tentative – even speculative – as they are considered, studious and prayerfully written. Though all writing inevitably ends with a full stop, these pages are faith seeking understanding, and so they are part of the question, 'What does it mean to be human, spiritual and Christ-like?', rather than a definitive answer.

As the title of the book suggests, this isn't a quick-fix, self-help spirituality for a consumer-driven culture, but a *permanent becoming* towards something that is, hopefully, a little more earthy, resourceful, and culturally attuned. It is a search for God, love, happiness, wholeness, purpose, social justice, environmental concern and faith in the midst of doubt. Ultimately, it is the discovery that true spirituality and authentic Christ-likeness are ordinarily human.

Being Human – Becoming Like Jesus

While the first disciples had trouble believing that Jesus was God, it strikes me that many Christians today have trouble remembering that Jesus was a human being.

Certainly, many of the worship songs we sing about Jesus tend to have a rather divine, other-worldly feel about them. And we're not helped in our quest for the human face of Jesus when celluloid representations typically employ actors who have a look of transcendence about them, speak with ethereal voices, and never appear in front of a camera which hasn't had a soft-focus filter applied to its lens.

Tom Wright put it like this: 'The word became flesh, and the church has turned flesh back into words.'

Witty, but should we be worried?

Now, you could be forgiven for thinking that we have more important things to fret about than discussing Jesus' DNA. Surely it's better that we recognize Jesus' divinity rather than concern ourselves with a fleshly humanity that we can no longer see or touch? After all, lots of people are happy that Jesus once walked around the shores of the Sea of Galilee. The stumbling-block is believing that this same historical Jesus is also the Second Person of the Divine Trinity. Isn't that one of the key things that sets us apart and defines us as Christian?

Well, as one of my old theology lecturers used to say: 'You're right in what you affirm, but you're wrong in what you deny.'

The thing is, when God created us, he created us as human beings. And he wants to keep us that way. Whoever we are, whatever we're going to be, we are going to become that as a flesh-and-blood human being, just as God intended. We're not encased in skin as a stopgap. We're not spiritual beings trapped in a human body – though that idea has plagued Christianity down the years. Even accepting biblical language about a 'new' humanity and 'resurrection' bodies, we're not prototypes. God didn't make a mistake or pick up the wrong mould when he formed us out of the dust of the earth. Human is what we are and human is what we're going to stay. So, we'd better get used to it.

The problem is, we're not doing this human thing the way God intended it to be done – and most of us intuitively understand this, even if we don't use spiritual or theological language in trying to express our unease at the way things are with us and the world.

We feel disconnected, from ourselves, from other human beings, from the creation and (for some of us at least) from God.

Which brings us nicely to the importance of Jesus' humanity.

If we want to know what humanity looks like . . .

If we want to understand the way humanity was meant to be according to God's creative purposes . . .

If we want to get back that connection with others and the creation – and God . . .

If we are going to have restored to us the opportunity to live and move and be who we are,[3] as anticipated in the creative imagination of God . . .

Then we need Jesus to be fully, authentically human, as God intended – otherwise, we're stuffed.

One of the earliest Christian thinkers said something like this: 'What isn't assumed, can't be redeemed.'

What he meant was this: For God to work out his plan to restore humanity to the original design brief, God had to become one of us; to make the change from within, not from without.

Kenosis

Of course, the elephant in the room is the one we're good at spotting: Jesus *was* God (the Second Person of the Divine Trinity) – and we're not. That's why we worship him.

Now I have to tread carefully here, for when you start to play around in the murky waters of Christology (trying to fathom the nature of Jesus/Christ), particularly the relationship between his human and divine natures, it's all too easy to get out of your depth and end up swimming into that theological maelstrom – heresy. So, I aim to keep firmly in the shallows.

The problem is this. Jesus managed to be authentically human, as we are meant to be. But, if he employed his divine nature to help him out with this small task, then that doesn't leave us with much hope of achieving the same feat – not being God, you understand.

So, here's the way it works:

When Jesus took on human nature, he chose not to play the God card, and all that came with that privilege, even though he remained fully God.[4] Rather, he laid aside the prerogatives associated with being God and relied instead on his relationship with God the Father and the Spirit of God, to be human.

Let's try that another way: Jesus lives a fully authentic human existence, doing all the things he does, not because he's God (though he is that), but because he's a human being living out his humanity in full, uninterrupted relationship with God and empowered to do so by the Holy Spirit.

Or to put it another way, Jesus is saying to us: 'I'm human, just like you. But, unlike you, I've got my relationship with God and the cosmos sorted out.'

Take the beginning of Luke's Gospel:

'The Holy Spirit *came down upon him . . .'*

'The Holy Spirit *was with him, and . . . led him into the desert . . .'*

'Jesus returned to Galilee with the power of the Spirit *. . .'*

'Jesus went . . . to the meeting place on the Sabbath . . . and read, "The Lord's Spirit *has come to me . . ."*'[5]

You see, Jesus isn't trying to play a game with us, or pull the wool over our eyes. He's not pretending to be Clark Kent, when secretly he's Superman. He's being human, but clearly there's something about the way he's doing this human thing that's setting him apart. Jesus appears to have got the whole thing sorted in a way we never quite seem to manage. Despite the fact that we humans are clearly advancing scientifically, medically and technologically at a great rate of knots, we don't (and never will) have the power, skill or ability to create for ourselves a genuinely new, good or eternal life without the loving intervention of God.

Without God, we are heading back into the chaos and nothingness that preceded God's creative act. However, just as the Spirit of God brought forth goodness out of the chaos of the raging seas (Hebrew, *tehom*),[6] so God's Spirit can bring forth true human spirituality and Christ-likeness out of the 'chaos' of our lives.

The important thing we need to grasp in all of this is that this 'better way of being human' is going to be made possible for us by Jesus, through the Spirit. We're going to get the chance to become human, just like Jesus, in just the same way – via our relationship with the Spirit.[7]

Earthy spirituality
Being clear about the humanity of Jesus also helps us in that characteristically twenty-first-century desire – to be 'spiritual'.

Like most things these days, spirituality has become just another dimension of our consumerist society. While some people think of themselves as spiritual, many of us simply think of ourselves as more 'rational' and 'pragmatic' – less in touch with our 'spiritual side'. What's more, because spirituality is now a choice, we can choose whatever spirituality takes our fancy and makes us feel good, fitting it into our 'life' the best we can. The problem is, this attitude not only devalues spirituality, it also devalues humanity. Spirituality shouldn't simply be considered an optional extra, for it is a necessary part of what it is to be a whole, God-intended human being.

> In the beginning . . . God took a handful of soil and
> formed a human body. Then God breathed into this body
> and gave it a life that reflected God's own.[8]

It is God's breath (Spirit) which brings life to our flesh and bones. Therefore, to call ourselves human is at one and the same time to recognize our spiritual nature. Our humanness is spiritual and our spirituality should celebrate that reality. Our thoughts, feelings, friendships, skills, creativity, imagination, work, family – all these things are very human. So, the mother or father who models Godly love to their child, or the person who cares for the sick and dying, or lobbies governments on behalf of the oppressed and voiceless – these people are as spiritual as any priest, monk or religious leader.

Spiritual life is not an escape from, or an overcoming of the bodily life; rather, it is living the way God intended, through every dimension of our bodies – physical and emotional. In other words, we don't have to become something we are not in order to be spiritual.

'Blessed are the poor in spirit'[9] – for even in their 'poverty' they are still recipients of God's life-giving Spirit.

As the Creation Story suggests, we receive life, but only after our bodies have been fashioned from more temporal elements. It shouldn't surprise us, then, that our spirituality is intended to reflect the earthiness of our being.

That's also why it's vital that we don't play down the human nature of Jesus. If Jesus becomes simply divine for us (a 'God' to be worshipped for what he has done), then he has become the opposite of incarnation – whatever that might be. What's more, we are so taken up with this worship of an absent, outside-of-time-and-place Jesus, that we become 'too heavenly minded to be any earthly good', as preachers are fond of telling us.

As with us, Jesus' body was a mass of sinews and cells. Not only that, but he was purposefully placed into a specific time and place and enabled to respond to it by the Spirit of God. If we ignore this, or fail to see the implications of it, we diminish the questions raised by Jesus' life that relate to culture and to politics, social justice and environmental concerns. What's more, these become irrelevant instead of central to our search for a genuine, authentic, human spirituality.

Jesus defines spirituality because he is dynamic in the Spirit.

Because of Jesus' incarnation, those things that are so often associated with spirituality – prayer, meditation, belief, faith, the search for enlightenment and truth – can never be permitted to have a life independent of the realities of human existence – of 'real' people, places and situations.

As Jesus said, if you're going to pray, pray this: 'On earth as it is in heaven' – those things that define God's living-space (peace, love, justice, mercy, wholeness, renewal, etc.), let those things be part of our world.[10]

We need to constantly remind ourselves that a truly transformative spirituality occurs through the ordinariness of everyday life. True spirituality is the anticipation of what might yet be, but lived out in the realities of the here and now, rather than an opportunity to take half an hour off from the painful realities of this world.

As the Jewish philosopher Martin Buber once said: 'Spirituality should lead you into the world, not lift you out of it.'

I know it's speculation, but I sometimes ponder this question: When God says, 'Be holy as I am holy',[11] does this mean 'set apart, other, distant, untouchable, pure, unapproachable'? Or does it mean, 'Be life as God is life' – whole, full, loving, relational, mutual, creative, connected, and so on?

What I have begun to understand (and this certainly isn't speculation) is this: we become ever more like Jesus, not by escaping the earth, but by burying ourselves deeper into the soil of life.

It's relationship, stupid!

Daniel Goleman, bestselling author of *Emotional Intelligence*, has got something of a theme going with his books. While writing this manuscript, I was reading one of Goleman's other offerings, *Social Intelligence* – catchy, hey! The subtitle for his work is this: 'The *new* science of human relationships' (emphasis mine).

To grossly over-simplify Goleman's argument: *We are made to connect*. More than that, *we create one another*. In other words, Goleman is giving credibility to the cheesy chat-up line: 'I need you. You complete me!'

It would seem the neurosciences are beginning to prove that we are affected by other people to a far greater degree than had previously been thought. Indeed, Goleman even suggests that certain types of genes are shaped by our context, environment and most importantly of all, the kinds of people we spend the majority of our time with – so, not just our emotions, but our very biology is relational.

Page after page, the book had this 'wow factor' going on for me – and then this light switches on in the dark void where my brain should reside. 'It's about relationships, stupid!'

- A Trinitarian God (three *Persons*, one essence *in relationship*).

- Adam in relationship with Eve because, 'It's not good being alone.'[12]

- The *Person* of the Spirit in relationship with the *Person* Jesus.

- Incarnation: God (a *personal* being) in human form relating to other *persons*.

New science, smew-science! This stuff is as old as the hills. Actually, it's as old as the God who made the hills!

But rather than dump the book, right there and then, I kept on reading this scientific narrative, but with the biblical story more to the fore – because, contrary to what some people would have you believe, the two worldviews aren't mutually exclusive.

More specifically, I read *Social Intelligence* with the Fruit of the Spirit in mind – because, if who I am (emotionally, intellectually, spiritually and biologically) is being impacted by other people with whom I share my life, then what effect is going to take place if I allow *the Person* (God) to enter my world through the Third Person of the Divine Trinity – the Spirit? A personal, divine being who just happens to be loving, happy, peaceful, patient, kind, good, faithful, gentle and self-controlled.

The Spirit is not just about being intelligent spiritually. It's about being socially intelligent, emotionally intelligent, intellectually intelligent, creatively intelligent, biologically intelligent. It's a holistic vision of what it means to be a human being. And all this comes out of the pleasure of being in relationship with Jesus through God's Spirit.

We become like Jesus, not by following some spiritual programme, but by developing a relationship with God and so, by the Spirit, produce that same fruitful human life that Jesus modelled. Therefore, the authenticity of our faith is best measured, not by our endurance in prayer, our regular church attendance, the quantity of money we give, or our grasp of the Bible, but by the Fruit of the Spirit, as evidenced by the quality of the relationships we have with God and others. For, if we love one another as God loves us, then everyone will know that we are connected to Jesus in some meaningful way.[13]

We shouldn't simply be trying to foster an *experience* of the Spirit, but rather we should be seeking a radical formation, a shaping and moulding of our lives so that we become ever more like Jesus. Our characters become spiritually coloured by our relationship with Jesus through his Spirit. Not just for our own benefit, but for the benefit of our family and friends and for the benefit of the complete stranger.

Goleman writes this: 'The social responsiveness of the brain demands that we be wise, that we realise how not just our moods, but our very biology is being driven and moulded by the other people in our lives – and in turn, it demands that we take stock of how we affect other people.'

Jesus said this: 'Love others, as much as you love yourself.'[14]

Paradox
One of the questions that's been bugging me while writing this book is how far the Fruit of the Spirit is simply a matter of the Spirit's presence in our lives, and how much I must get my hands dirty and do some cultivating?

You could easily be forgiven for thinking that it's pretty much a 'let go, and let God' arrangement. As Jesus seems to say when playing around with some fruity metaphors – 'Get yourself grafted into me, hang around off the true vine, and you'll produce some good grapes.'[15]

But I think the danger is that we push the whole metaphor too far. Metaphors have an 'is' and 'is not' quality about them. God 'is' a rock in the sense that he has a strength that can become the foundation of your life. But God 'is not' a rock in the sense that he is not cold, grey and inanimate.

So, while it's true that fruit appear on the vine simply because they are part of it, the Fruit of the Spirit has seeds of paradox within: 'Do *your* best to improve *your* faith . . . *by adding*'[16] . . . things that look remarkably like the Fruit of the Spirit!

While Jesus speaks of vines and fruit, he uses the idea of following him a lot more – and that feels a little more pro-active from our side of the bargain.

Again, I guess something of the answer lies in the understanding that we have a relationship with the Spirit of God that has some mutuality about it. Like any relationship, we can receive positive things by simply being in it. But if we really want the relationship to bear fruit, then we're going to have to work at it.

As one writer in the Bible put it: '*You* work out . . . because God is working in you.'[17]

Provided we recognize this mutual balance of receiving and responsibility, none of us should get discouraged. None of us should despair of ever becoming like Jesus and so being able to live that authentic human life we crave, because through his Spirit, God is ceaselessly at work in the world, shaping people into the likeness of Jesus.

'God is the one who began this good work in you, and . . . he won't stop before it is complete.'

Love Is . . . As Love Does

I'm sat watching one of Rob Bell's 'Nooma' DVDs. It's freezing cold and Rob's unloading gas canisters from the back of a 4x4 while unpacking some thoughts about the Old Testament poem, the Song of Songs. I'm captivated by this guy's teaching. Who wouldn't be?

Then, in a bemused, questioning tone, he says this: 'We'll tell somebody that we love them and in the same breath, we'll talk about how much we love a new car, or a certain pair of trousers. I mean – I love my wife, and I also love tacos?!'

I'm reading *Alice Through the Looking Glass*. Humpty Dumpty says this: 'When I use a word, it means just what I choose it to mean – neither more nor less.'

Human beings create language. And we create meaning out of language. We 'name' the world and its contents with language. But language shifts around in time and place. It changes. So does what we mean when applying it.

'I'm wicked,' but I'm not what you think I mean.

With language we play games. Many words can be used to describe the same idea. A single word can be adapted to express many thoughts. Some things in life we can define with ease. Other things evade capture, slip away from us even as we grasp after them. . . . We use words to speak about God.

Here's that word again: love.

And love is . . .?

It's not such an easy question, is it?

Love is many things, to many people. It's an emotion. An act of the will. It's romance. It's sexual intercourse. It's fleeting. It's lifelong. It's the topic of millions of song lyrics and myriad poems and novels. And yet it is neither summed up nor exhausted by any of these. Perhaps we've used the word 'love' so much in our culture that it has become meaningless and devalued.

Love has come to mean everything – so now it means nothing.

Actually, I don't think it's meaningless to say that I love my wife and I love tacos. I don't think I've devalued the word 'love', or my love for my wife, Kay, if I also say that I love my car, or the plum-coloured shirt she bought me for my birthday. When I say I love raspberry-ripple ice cream, I'm using the word 'love' to suggest that I have an extreme like for this particular flavour. Equally, to say I have an extreme like for Kay wouldn't be a false statement, it's simply not the entire picture when I say that I love her. I have something more complex and fuller in mind – which I'm sure will be reassuring to her!

Some people see the picture of me on my blog and say, 'Hey Alan, has anyone ever told you that you look like Rob Bell?' I don't. But I do *think* like Humpty Dumpty. I know what *I mean* when I tell my wife that I love her. I can differentiate in my mind (and in my soul) between my love for Kay and the desire I felt to have raspberry ripple for dessert. What's more, I can even distinguish between the subtleties and nuances of my love for Kay, my love for our daughter, and the love I have for friends – or my love for God, for that matter.

I guess the question is: Does my wife understand that my love for her is different to my love for anyone (or anything) else? Because of who I am, and the way I relate and express myself, does Kay feel loved and know she is loved uniquely, even if in the same breath I say I love tacos? And can the same be said for my daughter, my friends, my parents, my brother and sister, nephew and nieces?

Though it is but one word, 'love' isn't a single thing. It's a complex, not easily defined, hard-to-put-into-words phenomenon of human life. When we love, we are not actually trying to undertake a solitary enterprise, but an innumerable amount of things all at the same time.

The problem isn't that love has become meaningless. The problem is that it is so meaning-full that we are lost for words – except one: love.

Having said all this, thanks to Humpty Dumpty, we do have a problem when it comes to love, precisely because, when I use the word 'love', it means just what I choose it to mean – neither more nor less.

> But, where does that leave us when we read that 'The Fruit of the Spirit is love'?[19]

> What did the author intend to say when he wrote that the Fruit of the Spirit is love?

> Is the writer defining love here, or do I get to do that when I read it?

Perhaps God might like a say as to what love is.

Pure
God is love.[20]

The Christian theologian Emil Brunner said this was 'The most daring statement that has ever been made in human language.'

Given the complexities and possibilities for confusing the meaning and interpretation of the word 'love', it's very daring indeed. It's one thing to believe God is love. It's quite another to understand what God means by love. What if, down the road somewhere, human beings distorted God's idea of what love is. The statement 'God is love' no longer means what it's supposed to mean. And, once something is distorted, it can't un-distort itself. It needs something, or someone from the outside, to re-align it, to restore its intended shape. To remodel it. To heal it. To redeem it.

Thankfully, God's not naive. He knows language can only ever be an accommodation, an approximation, and that meaning can become evasive and philosophical. That's why the beauty of this revelation isn't in the imposing, evocative words, 'God' and 'love' – ideas that human beings have rightly played with via simile and metaphor, poetry and prose, art and film, but in doing so have at times clouded reality.

The key lies, not in the words that strike us first, but in the little word that connects the two: 'is'.

I love. You love. We love. We are capable of the act of loving because God loved us first.[21]

But God *is* love. Love is not simply something of which God is capable. Love is what and who God is. Theologians would say: love is God's ontology. We would say: love is God's nature; love is God's essence; love is God's being. God is pure love. Undistorted. Unpolluted. Unclouded. Whatever else you want to say about God, it has to be filtered through and understood in relation to the fact that God is love.

As the theologian Karl Barth said: 'Everything else to do with God is simply repetition and amplification of this statement. All that God imagines and desires, what he says and what he does, starts and ends and is directed by his love.'

That means, not only that love defines who God is, but that God gets to define that love.

Whatever we say love is, God has the trump card. Not that God wishes to dominate our language and expressions of love. But God is always there to say to us, 'Yes, but . . .'

'Yes, you love your family, but what about the poor of this world?'

'Yes, you love your friends, but what about the stranger?'

'Yes, you love those who love you, but what about those who despise you?'[22]

The fact that God is love should augment and transform all that human beings have to say and do in regard to love.

God *is* love. But that still hasn't explained what love is.

A verb

Because God is a personal being who is love, you cannot get to know that love by scientific experiment, or by theological or philosophical speculation. You can only know God's love whenever and wherever God makes that love known. And as the people of Israel discovered, love is made known by what God does: 'I am the Lord your God, the one who brought you out of Egypt, where you were slaves.'[23]

But when it comes to love, God doesn't stop there.

God so loved the world, that he didn't stay distant, making random acts of kindness. God isn't the kind of lover who sends the occasional card and bunch of flowers in token gesture of his love.

'God so loved the world that he gave his Son.'[24] God's love is made known in the world by incarnation. Love is embodied. Love dwells. The philosophical question, 'What is love?' becomes an anthropological one, 'Who is love?' And there can only be one answer to that question: Jesus.

Jesus said: 'If you have seen me, you have seen God.'[25]

Jesus could equally have said: 'If you have seen me, you have seen love.'

Jesus anchors love within his own Person.

But what does it mean to embody love?

Here are two complementary opinions:

'Greater love has no one than this, that he lay down his life for his friends.'[26]

'We know what love is because Jesus gave his life for us.'[27]

Clearly, here the cross of Jesus is in full view. But pull back from this apex of Jesus' love and you see a vista – a life that defined the statement, 'God is love.'

In the person of Jesus, love is cemented into action. Love is no longer a noun, naming something or somebody – even God. It's not some esoteric idea to contemplate. Rather, it becomes a *verb* – an active force. Love becomes real. Love is, as love does.

> Jesus . . . went to the meeting place on the Sabbath . . . was given the book of Isaiah . . . and read: 'The Lord's Spirit has come to me, because he has chosen me to tell the good news to the poor. The Lord has sent me to announce freedom for prisoners, to give sight to the blind, to free everyone who suffers, and to say, "This is the year the Lord has chosen."'[28]

This is Jesus' mandate for love. This is the blueprint for what love should look like. It's not exhaustive, but it is suggestive and broadly defining of what it means to love. It's Jesus' own commentary on his life and who he was – and he was and is, love.

As anyone familiar with the Gospels knows, Jesus healed the sick, liberated the oppressed, fed the hungry, consoled the sorrowful. He lived and died for others. This is Jesus expressing love as it should be expressed. Love as God intends. Jesus seeks to achieve goodness for others, rather than simply hoping for it. Jesus didn't say, 'I love everyone', meaning that he had a generally warm disposition towards people. He loved specifically and actively, and in so doing, generated well-being in the lives of other people.

Jesus exemplifies that great song of love, 1 Corinthians 13:

> *Jesus is kind and patient, never jealous, boastful, proud or rude.*
> *Jesus isn't selfish or quick-tempered.*
> *Jesus doesn't keep a record of wrongs that others do.*
> *Jesus rejoices in truth but not in evil.*
> *Jesus is always supportive, loyal, hopeful and trusting.*
> *Jesus never fails.*

At this point, I'm not just feeling good about Jesus, but I'm beginning to feel good about myself. I'm thinking, I love like Jesus. The love I have for others has the desire to become active. I feel the need to express myself when it comes to love.

I want the best for my partner.
I work at generating well-being for my daughter.
I desire and seek goodness for my friends and family.
I actively serve in my church and local community.
I even campaign on behalf of the poor and marginalized.

But Jesus hasn't finished defining love, yet: 'If you only love someone who loves you, will God praise you for that? Even sinners love people who love them . . . love your enemies and be good to them.'[29]

In saying this, Jesus isn't questioning whether our love is genuine or not. Jesus is raising the questions: Is your love defined by the God who is love? Is your love a fruit of your own spirit, or the fruit of God's Spirit?

The reality is, most of us love for selfish reasons. We love in the hope of being loved in return, because to give love out, but not have it returned, is at times a painful way to live. How common is the ache of unrequited, unreciprocated and unanswered love. Certainly, my teens and twenties are littered with broken relationships and the offering of my love to those who didn't want it. But then, I've also rejected the love that others offered me.

The Spirit takes human love to another level – to Jesus' level of love. It's a boundary-breaking love that empowers us to keep on loving when our love is scorned and rejected.

The Fruit of the Spirit is love – and that includes opening for us the possibility of loving those we feel don't deserve our love. As the Orthodox theologian John Zizioulas has said, Spirit-enabled love is 'without exclusiveness'.

I Love to worship

Jesus said: 'I tell you to love each other, as I have loved you.'[30] Which means that there is a necessary correlation between faith in Jesus and loving others. Actually, if we say we love God and don't love each other, we are liars[31] – strong stuff!

Loving others is our way of saying thank you, of worshipping God. Just as the worshipping community of Israel kept the Law of Moses as a way of saying thank you to God for freeing them from slavery in Egypt, so Christians should love others as an act of worship because Jesus has loved us.

'Thank you for saving me. What can I do?' Well,

> When I was hungry, you gave me something to eat, and when I was thirsty, you gave me something to drink. When I was a stranger you welcomed me, and when I was naked, you gave me clothes to wear. When I was sick you took care of me, and when I was in jail, you visited me.

When?

> *Whenever you did it for any of my people, no matter how*
> *unimportant they seemed, you did it for me.*[32]

In truth, 'love' is a word rarely directed at Jesus in the writings of the New Testament. The emphasis is nearly always on our love for others made possible by God's love for us through Jesus. So, why is it then, that so much worship is focused on words that say: 'Jesus, I love you'?

The truth is, our devotion to God is validated, not by words we sing but by our love for other people, because other people need our love as much, if not more, than God does. Why? Because human life withers when denied love, but God's life doesn't, due to the eternal love that exists within the divine communion of the Trinity.

Who can forget the children in Romanian orphanages after the collapse of communism? See what happens to a human life when it is starved of love and deprived of physical contact. Thank God that love finally came to those orphans which was gentle and kind, full of goodness and joy. For such love is spiritual, emotional and physical medicine.

A prism

Love is at the centre of God and the centre of Jesus' ministry. Everything spins out of and away from this centre.

Love is the hub at the heart of the universe. It's more important than anything else. It is what ties everything together.[33]

And this primacy extends to the Fruit of the Spirit.

It's no coincidence that love is first on the list when it comes to the Fruit of the Spirit. Without love we cannot hope to produce joy, peace, patience, kindness, goodness, faithfulness, gentleness or self-control, because such things are simply further expressions of the one, all-encompassing fruit: love.

When I worked for the Christian development organization, Oasis, I had one of those personality tests that assesses your strengths. It turns out that I thrive on mental activity; that I am attuned to the emotions of those around me; that I can see the potential in others and that I'm inquisitive and love to learn. The purpose in doing this test was to develop my strengths and to shape my role as an employee so as to maximize my usefulness.

But the Fruit of the Spirit isn't part of a personality test. It's not a list of strengths that I may or may not have, according to my disposition: 'Oh, I can do kindness, but I've never been very patient. I think it's a sign of intelligence or something.'

To put it another way: We can't turn the Fruit of the Spirit into a GM crop that's had faithfulness, patience and self-control genetically removed just because our culture struggles so much with these virtues.

The Fruit of the Spirit is an all-or-nothing, pips, peel, juice and flesh experience.

It's love expressed as Jesus expressed it – and Jesus' love expressed the full range of the Fruit of the Spirit, even when life wasn't a walk in the park.

More than one writer has likened love to light. Not an inappropriate metaphor, when you consider that Jesus has been described as the light that shines on everyone.[34] And when you shine light through a prism, what you see is the rainbow – the spectrum of colours that make up white light.

In the same way, if you could pass love through a prism, it would generate its own spectrum: joy, peace, patience, kindness, goodness, faithfulness, gentleness, self-control.

The Fruit of the Spirit is love – the rest is commentary.

The Joy in Happiness

Christians like to be different.

Sometimes, this can mean that we are interesting; that we've got something to say that makes people sit up and listen. A fresh take on life that draws people to Jesus. A way of being in the world that appeals to those who are looking for an alternative way to live, or that challenges injustices that clearly cut across God's purposes and intentions.

Sometimes, it means that we come across as better than everyone else. Holier than thou. Smug. Unappealing. We try to be different for the sake of difference. We call black 'white', even when we know it's black. We pointlessly distance ourselves from everyone else because . . . well, what has Alpha got to do with *Desperate Housewives*? – except for the fact that it's a series that's repeated all over the world.

Sometimes, we forget that we are human, just like everyone else. That we are all created in the image of God and that many of our needs and desires are basic, primitive, just the same as everyone else's needs and desires, because underneath our sophisticated front, that's the way we are.

Sometimes, our message has the potential to be so relevant to contemporary life that you can almost taste it. And then we go and make it irrelevant by suggesting that it's exclusive, rather than universal.

Take joy.

Joy is an aspect of the Fruit of the Spirit.

Which means, it must be special.

Which makes it different.

Which means, joy can't be the same as that common pursuit of the world: happiness.

While everyone else is running around like headless chickens, seeking out pleasure, grasping after a shallow, circumstance-driven, hedonistic, consumerist, fleeting commodity, we've got 'joy' – permanent and profound, deep and dependable, transcendent and spiritual.

And that makes us different – doesn't it?

Humpty Dumpty strikes again

One Sunday morning, my friend Pete Mansfield, said this:

'Why do we pretend that joy is somehow different to happiness? It strikes me, you can't be joyful unless you're happy. They are words that fit together. Joy is happiness that's been agitated. Un-agitated happiness is contentment. So, when I say joy, I mean happiness, and when I refer to happiness, I also mean joy.'

That's a good point. Are joy and happiness two different things, or are they the same thing? Is this a case where Christians are just trying to be different for the sake of being different? Are we talking ourselves into being completely irrelevant when we could be so on message? Are we messing around with semantics (what words mean), just to look clever?

In order to differentiate you have to define. You have to say, 'this word means this, while this word means that'. But according to all the dictionaries I own, 'joy' is a feeling of great happiness, and 'happiness' is feeling or showing pleasure, contentment or joy.

Not much differentiation there, then!

That means, in order to make the argument stick (that joy is somehow better than happiness), you have to say, 'What we mean by joy is something entirely different to what you mean when you say that you want to be happy.' And that's just what Christians tend to do.

They say things like, 'Happiness is dependent on circumstances. Circumstances change and so happiness is gone. Joy – well, that's a Fruit of the Spirit. It's of God. Who never changes. QED: joy is different to happiness.'

OK, but here's the problem. What if, when people say happiness, they mean (more or less) the same as what Christians mean when we speak about joy? What if, on paper, our culture's pursuit of happiness looks the same as our desire to produce that Fruit of God's Spirit which we call joy? What if we are actually singing from the same song-sheet, but there's simply been a typo, or an error in translation?

The truth is, when it comes to the relationship between 'joy' and 'happiness', it's not a different meaning that we should be seeking, but a fuller understanding.

Wake-up call

The search for happiness has a long history.

One ancient Greek philosopher said something like, 'No one ever pursues happiness as a means to something else.' By which, he meant that while you might go after money, or fame, or sex because you think they will bring you happiness, you don't go after happiness to get . . . well, you don't.

The point is this: the pursuit of happiness is core to who we are. It's one of the things that all human beings do. Happiness is a uniquely desirable commodity and the ultimate goal of many people's lives.

Observations like these led the not so ancient (and not so Greek) philosopher Jeremy Bentham to say something like: 'The best society is one where its citizens are happy. So the best thing a government can do is try and generate the greatest happiness for the greatest number of people.'

Bentham called his idea Utilitarianism – which won't make you happy.

But, hard to believe as it is, most government policy is simply trying to make as many people happy as is possible – which is really nice of them. Except that it isn't working!

All the research and reports suggest that happiness levels in the richest nations of the world have barely changed over the last fifty years, despite huge increases in prosperity, while some of the poorest countries on the planet have the happiest people. The fact is, policies that are only concerned with wealth generation are distracting us from what really produces happiness.

Take the Polish man who awoke from a coma, which had lasted nineteen years. He'd slept through the fall of communism and the rise of the free-market economy in his country. When asked what he noticed had changed, he said: 'The shops are now full. People have lots of new things, like designer clothes and mobile phones. But they're not as happy as I remember them.'

It would seem that the political mantra, 'It's the economy, stupid!' isn't worth repeating.

Re-think

Like our comatose Polish friend, people are waking up to the fact that 'having' and 'happiness' aren't necessarily related. The psychologist Martin Seligman says 'happiness' comes in two forms: 'Pleasant Life' and 'Good Life'.

Pleasant Life – well that's the kind of happiness that people try to build via materialism and hedonism. It's me-centred, and driven by the desire for immediate gratification. In short: It's the belief that possessions and sensual experiences will produce happiness. It's about desire rather than what we actually need. It relies on people implicitly believing that happiness can be bought. It perpetuates the idea that happiness is derived from the pursuit of pleasure – and that's been a common mistake throughout human history.

Not that there is anything necessarily wrong with pleasure. We are, after all, sensual beings. Money, sexual intimacy and having new stuff do make us happy – just not for very long. What's more, they can at times get in the way of things that generate happiness that lasts.

The problem lies here: people confuse pleasure with happiness. And it's pleasure that's fleeting, not happiness.

So, if it's happiness rather than pleasure we are ultimately pursuing, then we need to look elsewhere to satisfy that core human need.

Enter the Good Life.

The Good Life is about true happiness – a permanent reality in spite of life circumstance.

(Wait a minute! Isn't that what Christians say joy is?)

The Good Life recognizes that there are factors that can generate core happiness, which isn't vulnerable to the vagaries of our consumerist culture. There are universals that produce happiness in all times and in all places.

That's not to suggest that happiness is a constant that has no ebb and flow to it. It's not static. It changes over the course of a lifetime as it responds to our circumstances. But happiness can remain with us as a foundation of who we are even when life becomes tough.

Indeed, many people manage to be happy despite severe illness, disability or poverty. The truth is, such things do not automatically condemn us to persistent unhappiness, just as wealth and good looks won't necessarily bring us joy.

Equally, to look after a loved one who is sick, or to comfort those who mourn, may not be a pleasurable experience. We may not even 'feel' happy about having to do this. But that doesn't mean it has nothing to do with happiness. Indeed, involvement with someone's suffering, tending to their needs – be they emotional or physical – can connect us to them in a deep way. And human connectedness, even in the midst of pain and sorrow, is a building-block to happiness.

The R-factor

Paul Martin, author of *Making Happy People*, is clear that there is no single golden key to happiness, and never will be. Many different ingredients contribute to the development of happiness, and the same outcome can be reached via many different routes.

But he's equally clear that one factor comes up time and time again: relationships.

The relationships we have and cultivate are (for better or for worse) the single biggest influence on happiness. Ordinary, everyday people are our joy. Not iPods, widescreen HDTV, holidays abroad, fast cars, or good wine and fine food. Independent of the people who share our lives, stuff is nothing more than a passing pleasure.

Beyond the basic requirements of food, warmth and shelter, material wealth is not a fundamental human need. But, being connected with other people is. And yet, we often live out our contemporary lives as if it were the other way around.

The mobile and fragmented nature of urban society means that many individuals are no longer part of a tightly-knit network of family, relatives and close friends. Someone living in a city might interact with hundreds of people every day while commuting, working, shopping, watching sport or going to the cinema, and yet have no meaningful connection with anyone. So we fill the gap with other 'things'.

It's a sad reality of modern life that many of us are economically well off, but relationally very poor. At times, we can feel desperately lonely, despite being immersed in a sea of humanity.

And as Mother Teresa noted: 'There is no greater poverty than loneliness.'

And, just to rub salt into the wound, it's this relational poverty that the advertising industry exploits within the post-industrialized, affluent societies of the West. They know what really makes us happy. That's why cars and alcohol, insurance and clothing, air fresheners and ready meals are all directly associated with love, close friendships, freedom and other genuine sources of happiness. Yet in reality, personal relationships, which make a huge contribution to our happiness, have little, if anything to do with alcohol or air fresheners.

What's more, without meeting our real need for meaningful, happiness-generating relationships, the aspiration for material possessions escalates. The more we have, the more we want. The pleasure of what we already have fades, so we need more pleasure from more stuff. The more our neighbour has (who we don't really know), the more we feel we need.

Stop! There will always be people who are richer, better looking, and more famous than you are. I, for one, need no convincing of that argument.

So, if you're going to buy anything, then buy into this: the support, confidence and emotional security that come from close personal relationships form the bedrock of happiness.

The G-factor

OK. I admit it. You can only go so far with this happiness thing before you have to mention God. But the point I'm trying to make is this: the G-factor informs and deepens our understanding and pursuit of happiness rather than replacing it with something unique and altogether different.

As John Ortberg once wrote: 'We will never understand the significance of joy in human life until we understand its importance to God. . . . God is the happiest being in the universe.'

But then, why wouldn't he be?

For a start, he's got the key element sorted: God has quality, mutual relationship within his own being – Father, Son and Spirit.

Which means, God is generating happiness out of his own self.

Which means, Jesus' joy comes from his relationship with the Father and the Spirit.[35]

Which means, the Fruit of the Spirit is happiness if for no other reason than it comes out of a relationship with God.

Flow

God's got another happy factor going on: he's outward-looking and gains satisfaction in what has been described as 'flow' – an ability to be absorbed in something other than one's own self. And what God is absorbed in is you, me and the rest of his creation. Which is a staggering and humbling thought.

What's more, God's 'flow' means that creation is an expression and perpetuation of God's happiness. Indeed, creation itself responds with joy as 'Desert pastures blossom and mountains celebrate. Meadows are filled with sheep and goats; valleys overflow with grain and echo joyful songs.'[36] The connectedness of the creation to the Creator makes it joyful – and we are part of that creation, which is why one of the Fruit of the Spirit is happiness.

I think children are often closer to the image of God than adults when it comes to generating happiness from creation. Perhaps they are too young to be disconnected by human exploitation of the world in which we live. Or, possibly they're just better at seeing the goodness that's around them, and enjoying the wonder of what God has given them. Either way, they seem to tap into the joy and happiness of simply being alive in ways that many adults don't.

I'm trying to regain wonder through my daughter. She can see the moon and burst into dances of delight, or be captivated by shadows or the sensation of sand running through her fingers. I even recall taking her to the zoo, trying to be exuberant about the lions and gorillas, but she was transfixed by something more mundane – a park-keeper sweeping up autumn leaves.

Be absorbed beyond yourself. Connect with nature. Feel the joy that's still there, despite the ravages of human activity. Sense the numinous and transcendent qualities within the universe. Be happy.

The end of happiness

Because happiness exists eternally within the Trinity, and because it is at the heart of the creation, it has a trajectory through time and space.

Yes, happiness is at the beginning of creation – but it is even more so at the end.

Which means that, while there is something very real, tangible and permanent about our happiness here and now, we must always hold onto the fact that it's becoming more. Our happiness is partial and incomplete. Therefore, we shouldn't mistake the already, with the not yet. Even the joy-filled creation isn't contented. It is looking to a time that's yet to be.[37]

Ultimately, happiness is about hope. It's eschatological, meaning it's future-orientated. It's about the end when 'God will make his home among his people. He will wipe tears from their eyes, and there will be no more death, suffering, crying, or pain. These things of the past [of our present] are gone forever.'[38]

Therefore, whatever situation, or life circumstance we find ourselves in, being future-orientated should bring forth happiness in the here and now by drawing it down from our futures. The hope of happiness systematically changes the way we view the world, bringing perspective into unhappy situations.

It brought perspective to God's people exiled in Babylon.[39]

It brought perspective to Jesus as he faced the suffering of the cross.[40]

It brought perspective to the early Christians suffering under Roman oppression.[41]

So, it should bring us perspective, also.[42]

Happiness hubs

One of the psalmists says this: 'Your people are wonderful and they make me happy.'[43]

Is church the first place you go to look for happiness?

Lots of people I know think Christians are joyless, when in reality, we should be leaders in the pursuit of happiness. We need big advertising hoardings outside our churches saying 'Happiness is Here!'

But that means the church has to walk the road that leads to happiness. We need to become living signposts for people to follow towards the Good Life. The elements that produce happiness should be at the centre of our Christian communities.

People are genuinely looking for a happiness that lasts. So let's tell them that they can find it with God, through God's Spirit, within the Christian community, and not play games by pretending that happiness is a worldly pursuit, while we have something altogether better, called joy.

The pursuit of happiness is a legitimate biblical, theological and sociological objective.

Here's some good advice from Paul Martin. It's not biblical. But that doesn't mean it isn't true or that you can't find the same advice in Scripture. Actually, I think God would say, 'Yes and Amen' to it. What's more, I think it's a great place to start if we want to make our Christian communities happiness hubs.

- Take a broad, long-term view of happiness: there is much more to it than immediate pleasure.

- Happiness is good for you, good for your children and good for society, so don't be embarrassed about making it a top priority.

- Personal relationships are absolutely central to happiness and health. Be connected.

- Be active and engaged: throw yourself into meaningful pursuits.

- Look outwards, not inwards: focus your attention on other people and the world around you rather than dwelling on your own thoughts and feelings.

- Love unconditionally.

- A good education is one that fosters, among other things, social and emotional competence, communication skills, wisdom, resilience and a lifelong love of learning.

- Let children play.

Doh!

I once wrote this:

> *We often interchange the words 'joy' and 'happiness' as if they are the same commodity. They are not. Happiness is dependent on your circumstances – do you like your job, has your relationship just ended, what's your financial situation? Joy is something much deeper.*

The beauty of life is that you live and learn, and sometimes you even get the chance to change your mind. And I'm changing mine.

The Fruit of the Spirit *is* happiness!

Peace, Imperfect Peace

I was born in the sixties.

I don't remember it (due to my young years, not my drug intake), yet it has entered my psyche.

A time for a Summer of Love. A time for Hippies. A time for Woodstock. A time for Mitchell, Baez and Dylan. A time to drop out. A time to wear flowers in your hair. A time to make love, not war. A time to protest against Vietnam.

There is a time for war and a time for peace.[44]

The seasons come and go.

I grew up in the seventies.

A time for strikes. A time for power cuts and a three-day week. A time for Glam Rock and a time for Punk. A time for Cold Wars. A time for four-minute warnings. A time to fear nuclear attack. A time for CND.

There is a time for war and a time for peace.

The seasons come and go.

I became a man in the eighties and nineties.

A time for Yuppies and a time for high unemployment. A time for 'loads o' money' and a time for none. A time for race riots. A time for Thatcher and Reagan. A time for New Romantics. A time for Live Aid (*I was there!*). A time for Brit Art and Brit Pop. A time for the Falklands conflict. A time for the Gulf War.

There is a time for war and a time for peace.

The seasons come and go.

I'll become middle-aged in the naughties.

A time for globalization. A time for YouTube and Facebook. A time for downloads and Arctic Monkeys. A time for global warming. A time for Live Earth. A time for Blair, Bush and Brown. A time for 9/11. A time for 7/7. A time for war on terror. A time for Afghanistan and Iraq. A time to say: 'Not in my name!'

A time for war and a time for peace.

The seasons come and go.

Pacifism

At any given time, there is conflict and there is peace in our world. These diametrically opposed states seem to find the space to co-exist on our planet. They always have, and I guess they always will – until peace finally wins out.[45]

Maranatha![46]

I'm not a fatalist, just a realist. And I guess I'm also a pacifist – though this has never been tested in the face of a true aggressor. But when I say 'pacifist', I have something more expansive in mind than simply meaning that I am opposed to the use of war as a means to settle disputes. Just as when God speaks of peace, he means something far more holistic than simply the cessation of conflict.

As a pacifist, I desire to actively live in a way that brings peace in line with God's idea of *shalom*.

Shalom. Peace. Not a negative state: the *absence* of war. But a positive one: the *presence* of God made manifest in every strata of creation. God's peace is an active-becoming, which moves the creation and humanity into the fullness that God intended from the moment when he first said, 'Let there be . . .'.[47]

A peace that he intended for the Covenant people of Israel.

A peace that Jesus spoke about and practised.

A peace that is concerned for environmental, social, economic, political, moral and individual well-being.

Shalom: creation
God created the world with peace in mind.

Some would say: 'In the beginning . . . God created peace out of raging chaos and conflict.'[48] What is clear is that the creation was full – abundant, blessed, fertile and purposeful. It was without enmity or strife. It was *shalom*.

From now on, to speak of peace was to recall this vision of God's creation.

When Aaron blessed the people of Israel, the words he used were these: 'May the Lord be good to you and give you peace.'[49] In so doing, Aaron was employing creation language: May the Lord give you *shalom*. May you know fruitfulness and abundance. May your lives be as purposeful as the God-intended creation and without enmity or strife.

When God's people were overrun and taken into exile (586 BC), the prophets evoked visions of a return to a land bursting with *shalom*, where . . .

> *Deserts will become orchards thick as fertile forest.*
> *Honesty and justice will prosper there,*
> *and justice will produce lasting peace and security.*
> *You, the Lord's people, will live in peace, calm and*
> *secure. . . .*
> *You will have God's blessing,*
> *as you plant your crops beside streams,*
> *while your donkeys and cattle run freely.[50]*

And always at the centre of this ongoing prophetic vision is the city where God's people dwell: Jerusalem: *Yerusha-shalom* or 'Inheritance of peace'.

> *I am creating new heavens and a new earth. . . .*
> *I am creating a Jerusalem, full of happy people. . . .*
> *There will be no more crying or sorrow in that city.*
> *No child will die in infancy; everyone will live to a ripe old age. . . .*
> *No one will take away their homes or vineyard. . . .*
> *I will bless their children and their grandchildren.*
> *I will answer their prayers before they finish praying.*[51]

> *God's home is now with his people. . . . He will wipe all tears from their eyes, and there will be no more death, suffering or crying or pain. These things are past and gone forever.*[52]

Shalom: Jesus

Read the Gospels through the lens that Jesus is the bringer of *shalom*, and they make perfect sense, because they are full of healing, words of fruitfulness and teaching about fulfilment and wholeness. Right from the off, Jesus is being placed into that overarching narrative that says that God's activity within human history is to be aligned with his vision of a creation existing as *shalom*.

'Peace is on earth,' announce the angels on Jesus' arrival.[53] *Shalom* is here, incarnate in human form.

Of course, Jesus isn't the only one claiming this.

Caesar Augustus liked to call himself 'the divine, son of god, saviour of the world, who brought peace to everyone'. But as someone once said: 'It's a strange kind of peace that comes by employing violence to achieve and maintain it.' In any case, God's people didn't want *Pax Romana*, they wanted God's 'In the beginning/behold, I make all things new' vision of peace.

And that's just what Jesus intends to provide. A distinctive, unique, undisputed, unmatched peace – *Pax Christus*: 'I give you peace, the kind of peace that only I can give. It isn't like the peace that this world can give. So don't be worried or afraid.'[54]

So, what did this vision look and sound like in the hands of Jesus?

It looks and sounds like an act of creation: order out of chaos. As if to conjure with one of the foundational stories of human history, Jesus moves across stormy seas just as God's Spirit did.[55] Not only that, but he speaks to the chaotic waters and says, 'Peace! Be still!'[56]

It's also the bringing forth of wholeness out of brokenness. Time and again we see Jesus intervene to restore the crippled, the lame and the disfigured. 'Get up! Pick up your mat and go home.'[57] Return from the 'exile' your body has placed you in and live in peace.

Jesus plays with images of abundance as if to say, 'I am the source of God's *shalom*.' He provides food within a desert place to feed thousands and still has more to offer.[58] And he says things like: 'I am the true vine, and you are the branches. If you stay joined to me, and I stay joined to you, then you will produce lots of fruit.'[59]

Those who are social outcasts, and filled with shame, are brought back into the heart of the community through Jesus' actions. So, he heals a man who has leprosy. But instead of sending him home, he sends him to a priest, so that his healing would be verified and recognized by all, allowing him to live once more with his family and friends. To be returned to the community.[60]

In similar vein, Jesus offers hospitality and fellowship around his table for those considered untouchable. He eats with the marginalized and disenfranchised, the blind, the sick and the lame, bringing into the here and now a taste of that great, end-of-time banquet that finally celebrates the realization of God's *shalom* throughout the cosmos.[61]

What's more, there's justice to be had, where there was once injustice. Instead of punishment at the hands of an angry mob, a woman caught in adultery hears these words from Jesus: 'If there is no one here to accuse you, then I will not condemn you.'[62]

But perhaps most striking and awe-inspiring of all, there is life where there once was death: '"I am the one who raises the dead to life! . . . Lazarus, come out!" And the man who had been dead came out.'[63]

Shalom: wage peace

I'm in a packed auditorium. Rob Bell is taking questions from the floor. Most people seem preoccupied with asking him what it's like being the pastor of a mega-church or how you get to grow such a large congregation.

I'm thinking, 'Probably not being so fixated with the idea would be a start.'

Thankfully, Rob's being more gracious than I am and he's answering these questions the best he can.

But I'm frustrated by the way things are going, so I get to my feet and ask: 'If Jesus were drafted in to advise Blair and Bush on the war in Iraq, what do you think he'd say?'

Here's the gist of Rob's answer: If you're blessed, then you've got to be a blessing to others. If you're blessed and people want to attack you, then you've got to be asking why they'd want to do that. People aren't generally aggressive unless they've been forced into a corner.

I accept that we can't prevent random acts of violence – evil will do what evil does. But much enmity has its roots in what *we* do and how *we* live. Those we oppress will eventually turn on the oppressor. And violent revolution tends to lead to further violence.

So, be peacemakers by living in such a way as not to create enemies. If you've tasted something of what it means to have peace, in its fullest sense, then you're privileged, and you're responsible for ensuring that others share in that foretaste of *shalom*.

Please don't mis-read this as an exercise in pointing fingers or the provision of an excuse for terrorism and violence. To do so would both deny the complexities of the global situation and fail to recognize that the vast majority of people who suffer poverty, injustice and abuse of their human rights do so with dignity and non-violence.

However, the current global situation does throw up two issues that get to the heart of God's ideals when it comes to *shalom*: *responsibilities* and *response*.

Responsibilities
If you're party to God's *shalom*, either in reality, or by being aware of the intended vision, then the deal is this: you're responsible to work with God to see it established, on earth as it is in heaven – to borrow some words from Jesus.

Irrespective of whether injustice, poverty and infringement of human rights are the cause of war, radicalization and violent revolution, the presence of such things in the world means that peace, in line with a biblical vision of *shalom*, is absent.

Shalom is all or nothing.

The prophets may well have brought visions of *shalom* to encourage the exiled people of Israel and Judah, but they also made it clear that peace isn't simply bestowed – it is earned. Human beings have responsibilities when it comes to bringing forth order out of chaos:

> No matter how much you pray, I won't listen.
> You are too violent.
> Wash yourselves clean!
> I am disgusted with your filthy deeds.
> Stop doing wrong and learn to live right.
> See that justice is done.
> Defend widows and orphans and help those in need.[64]

And what was true for God's people BC is even more so CE (which is supposed to be PC for 'AD' and means 'Common Era', but I'm going to use it here to mean after the 'Christ Event'), because when you've witnessed the duty that Christ felt to do what God impels all human beings to do in the face of poverty and injustice, then there's no other way to understand our responsibility when facing similar issues. As one New Testament writer puts it: 'When peacemakers plant seeds of peace, they will harvest justice.'[65]

As I said earlier, I am a realist, as we all should be. Peace, this side of Christ's return, is vain hope. At the very least because we will always have the poor with us.[66] But that's not a mission statement for pessimists. Rather, it's a nagging reminder of our responsibility to act, and to endeavour, and to strive for *shalom*.

Neither does realism preclude idealism. We are part of a continuum that will one day make poverty history; and witness the cessation of conflict; and see justice done; and see the creation renewed . . . and so we keep on keeping on. For wherever an injustice is set right, or an environmental victory is won, or reconciliation is achieved where there once was conflict (be that between friends, or at an international level), then the cause of peace is advanced.

Response

Shalom isn't just about our responsibilities. It is also *how* we respond on behalf of others, or indeed, on behalf of ourselves – for at times we all have to face poverty, injustice or the threat of conflict – even if that is simply on a personal level.

You could say, we have a responsibility to respond in line with Jesus' response.

If I'm honest, I'm not a very confrontational person. Anything for an easy life or to keep the peace. Perhaps that's because, in my younger years I had a lot of confrontation and fights, none of which turned out to be very pleasant experiences, even if I won.

As I get older, however, I'm beginning to understand that my failure to confront situations that demand a response other than backing down, walking away or keeping silent, isn't a pathway to peace either. In fact, the opposite is probably true.

If I don't respond, then the situation that is angering me gets played over and over again within myself.

At the very least, that means I have no peace. But it can also mean that at some stage there is the very real possibility that I will reach boiling point and respond in a way that not only serves to escalate the situation, but may result in actions that bring about further conflict or strife, rather than a peaceful resolution.

The truth is, the pursuit of peace does not include an easygoing peace-at-any-price attitude. It does not include capitulating to wrong or injustice so as to avoid doing what we know is right. Pursuing peace does not mean running away from the causes of discord, but rather, it means facing them head-on.

The peace campaigner and former hostage in Iraq, Norman Kember, once said that he was compelled to do something more than simply sign a petition or march on Whitehall or the White House with a banner proclaiming 'Not in My Name!' – important as those things are. For him personally, this was 'easy peace'. It wasn't really confronting the issue at hand. Neither was it enough of a radical alternative to the response of his government, which was to confront violence with violence. Norman believed there was another way – the way of God. The way of Jesus. The way of *shalom*.

Let's be in no doubt: Jesus was very confrontational. He confronts in order to bring about peace. He confronts distorted religious practices. He confronts distorted social, political and economic practices. Which means he confronted the aggressor of his time: Rome. Jesus also confronted the evil that lies behind such distorted structures and systems.

But let's also be in no doubt about this: Jesus never confronts such things with violence, because violence is anathema to *shalom*.

Turn the other cheek. Walk the extra mile. Love your enemies. Then you will be acting like God.[67]

Not that either God, or Jesus, simply capitulated, or acquiesced, in the face of injustice and violence. What you see in Jesus' life is a robust, creative and active engagement with everything that set itself over and against God's agenda of peace. For while Jesus' life was a peaceful protest against such things, it was also a protest full of peace. Or to put it another way, it realized the reality of peace, rather than just hoped for it.

Shalom: people

Much of what I've said here may seem rather grandiose: international conflict, global poverty and injustice, environmental concern. But if you recall what's been said in regard to Jesus, much of that was simply about reconciliation and peace between peoples in community.

Peace pervades. It is *shalom* for all, within every dimension of life.

I, for one, can find myself so wrapped up in what's going on halfway around the world, that I neglect to work for peace among my friends and family, and within my Christian community – even within my own soul.

But to call myself Christian is to recognize that I am part of a community that is constituted by God's Spirit and orientated around the cross of Jesus. And even though Jesus' cross is many things, it is without doubt a cross of peace. It reconciles us to God and makes peace between us.[68] But it also opens the way for us to be reconciled to each other, and to ourselves.[69]

The cross is atonement. At-one-with. Peace between. *Shalom*.

And that places a demand on us that we too become a people of peace and reconciliation; that we take up the purpose of the cross in our own lives.

When you take communion, offer each other a sign of peace. Not a wet handshake or a tentative hug. Offer each other a true sign of peace – *shalom*. Recall to mind Aaron's blessing. Envisage the first creation and the new creation. And envisage how you can bring this into each other's lives . . . and then act upon it.

Peace-building is a communal activity, not an individual pursuit.

For sure, many of us desire inner peace – I do too. But within this world, there are only two ways to achieve this. One of them is to adopt the worldview of an ostrich – sticking our heads in the sand, ignoring conflict, division, injustice and poverty, so that such things don't impinge on our conscience. Thereby we receive the peace of the ignorant individual. Which is not really peace.

The alternative is to adopt the worldview of *shalom*. To work with all our heart, mind and strength to bring about peace – even if that is only within our own little corner of the world. This way, we receive the peace that Jesus speaks about. We become peace-bringers, just as Jesus was. And we bear the Fruit of the Spirit, which is peace.

A PERMANENT BECOMING / Five

The Patience of a Sinner

When I was a child, titillating my primal fear by watching Dr Who save the universe from Cyber Men, Daleks and giant green maggots, the nice people at the BBC made you wait a whole week between episodes. There's Dr Who, sonic screwdriver in hand, trying desperately to escape from a locked room, Cyber Men closing in, the future of humankind in the balance and . . . well, you'll have to wait to discover Dr Who's fate, because he's not going to be back on until next Saturday teatime.

Now I'm older, I've got real fears to occupy me, so watching Dr Who tackle rubberized enemies doesn't have the same appeal. In any case, there's technically no cliff-hanger any more. So long as you have digital TV, you can simply switch over to another channel once the episode ends, and discover the outcome within two minutes . . . 'just in case you can't wait'.

But, wasn't waiting the point?

Didn't that build the tension and allow you opportunity to employ your imagination, to consider the Doctor's fate, to discuss the episode with your mates at school on Monday morning, to lay awake at night contemplating what you would do if you were Dr Who's assistant facing the same situation and how you would make your escape – that being the only certainty?

Haven't we lost more than we realize by doing away with the wait?

I guess running back-to-back episodes of *Dr Who* is simply symbolic of an obvious reality: our culture doesn't do patience.

What we do instead is . . .

Fast food. Everything from burgers to pre-prepared sandwiches, to pizzas, to ready meals, to vegetables that have been washed, peeled and sliced for you, to mashed potato that's ready to blitz for thirty seconds in the microwave, because making mashed potato must take all of twenty minutes; time I could be using to check my . . .

E-mails every few minutes, because normal post is 'snail mail' compared with . . .

Faster broadband speeds, which allow us to surf quicker to find the best deals on . . .

Credit and loans, because we can't wait to get our hands on the latest . . .

Technology, which moves at such a pace that we . . .

Dump millions of perfectly good mobile phones and computers and TVs every year just because the newest ones have got one more feature that ours doesn't have and which we're never going to use, but we're too embarrassed not to have because . . .

None of our peers can wait to have it, which teaches our children . . .

Pester power. Which is just a young person's version of 'I want it and I want it now', but children can't get credit or loans and so they have to manipulate mummy and daddy and use their borrowed money to buy pretty much the same things that adults want, which generates what psychologists call . . .

'Age-compression', which is basically shorthand for pre-pubescent children living like they've got a mid-life crisis and screaming, 'I don't won't to be a child and I can't wait to grow up!' because . . .

Well, nothing in our culture suggests there is any value in waiting.

Patience? That's a prison sentence, not a virtue!

Goldfish

Culture is the water in which we swim.

Ask a goldfish, 'Do you mind swimming around in a ten-inch glass bowl with multi-coloured gravel and a plastic mermaid for company?' and you're going to get a blank look, because the goldfish isn't really aware that this is it's 'culture'. It's just swimming along where it finds itself.

Now, drag to the side of the bowl a widescreen HDTV and put on a DVD of koi carp cruising around a four-by-five-metre pond complete with a range of aquatic plants, a water feature and a *faux* Japanese footbridge and . . .

Now the goldfish understands the question. Now it realizes that there is an alternative to the way life is; that there are 'cultures' other than its own. Suddenly, you've expanded the worldview of the goldfish. You've given it another story. There's contrast to consider. There's a 'stop and think' sign that's come into view.

Most of the time, we're just like the goldfish. We're swimming around within the culture in which we live and not really thinking about it. Why would we? With the pace of life as it is, we simply don't have time to sit and consider the detail. In any case, if we start navel-gazing there's every chance we are going to get left behind.

The pace of life – that's part of our culture.

But give yourself enough time to think about this: the unconsidered life is not worth living.

That was the opinion of Socrates.

To consider life is like inspecting a map before you set off on a journey, or occasionally stopping en route to make sure you're not lost and you're happy with the direction in which you're going. It also allows you to ask: Who's deciding the content of this life – me or the culture in which I live? What and who are influencing me?

Back in 2005, the BBC broadcasted a programme about five men who opted to take time out and spend a few weeks inside Worth Abbey, a monastic community in the heart of rural England. Which is a breeze, right?

Actually, it was like hardened drug users doing cold turkey, such was the contrast with the culture they were used to. Stripped of all the trappings of contemporary life, deprived of their technological comfort blankets, such as mobile phones and email accounts, these men were plunged into a way of life that was slow, considered and patient. And for some of them, the experience changed their lives.

God's culture

To encounter God, in the narrative of the Bible, through the life of Jesus, and via the Holy Spirit, is to encounter a contrast to our own culture. Not because such things are archaic and of the past. Only ignorance assumes that you can apply the past tense to God or Jesus, or confine them to a fairy story that starts with 'A long time ago, in a land far, far, away . . .'.

God, in Jesus, is the same yesterday, today and forever.[70]

Meaning, not that God is static and unchanging, but that he is active within creation at all times and in all places. The one who is, and was, and is coming.[71]

God is not the past, an archaic and primitive figment of human imagination, having little, if anything, to add to our contemporary world. God continually spills over into people's lives. Whatever comes and goes, whatever the changes that happen, God's ability to shape revelation into a form that is meaningful is never exhausted. Whatever the *zeitgeist* (the spirit or mood of the age), God's alternative culture breaks in with the words: 'I am the way, the truth and the life.'[72]

So it is with patience. Our culture may not see any value in the wait, or the virtue in patience. But God cuts across our goldfish-bowl mentality with a vision, a sign, or a story from another culture – God's culture – where the purpose and value of patience is known and realized.

More than that: God raises within us questions of possibility:

Can I embrace this alternative culture?

Am I able to dwell differently in this world?

Can I become all that God intended me to be?

A sudden rush of patience

To encounter God and his purposes is to encounter a culture of patience.

Though, of course, you don't necessarily always get that impression when reading the Bible. Take the opening couple of chapters, for example:

'In the beginning God created the heavens and the earth. . . .'[73]

God certainly appears to be in a hurry with this whole creation thing. After all, whatever we may feel about the actual timescales involved, the pace of the narrative races on at breakneck speed. It's a big bang of an opening. Where's the evidence of a patient God here?

Actually, it's built into the metanarrative, the bigger picture.

The creation may seem to happen all of a sudden, but how long had passed within the eternal nature of God before the instant moment of that first creative act? How long had God contemplated the creation in his divine imagination before setting stars in the heavens, pushing back the oceans to expose the land, and placing human beings into a garden planted in the east? What reads with pace, in reality transcends time and space. What's more, in its entirety, the biblical narrative assumes an origin from eternity, spreads itself over thousands of years of human history, before slipping back into eternity.

Once you actually get going into the story, you begin to see the God who is patient with his creation and his concern to redeem it, along with an estranged humanity. For while God is quick to make a covenant with, and a promise to, Abraham,[74] he does not rush it along. Not even Abraham sees the fulfilment of this undertaking in his lifetime.[75] A few hundred years later, we see Moses lead the Hebrew slaves (Abraham's descendants) out of Egypt – eventually.[76] Add another 1,500 years or so and the communities of Israel and Judah are exiled into Babylon, and then repatriated. Add a few hundred more, and Jesus finally comes onto the scene, despite the prophet Malachi ending what we call the Old Testament with the words: 'Then *suddenly* the Lord you are looking for will appear in his temple. The messenger you desire *is coming* with my promise, and *he is on his way*.'[77] As for when God will wrap the whole thing up so Jesus can 'come soon' (again) – well, that's anyone's guess. Despite the fact that some Christians have time-lines mapping the whole thing out!

So, while, 'Behold, I make all things new'[78] sounds like it's a sudden, instant reveal, or a cosmic 'Ta-dah!', it's actually been one of those slow-motion cinematic panning shots across time and space. It's actually the culmination of who knows how many years of what theologians call 'salvation history': the patient, ongoing purpose of God to renew the creation and restore our relationship with him.

All of creation awaits this 'moment' of the new creation. But then, to speak of a 'moment' in this context is irrelevant. It's suddenly an obsolete term. A word from the old order of things – the frustrating space–time order in which we still have to live, patiently waiting for God to make his move.

Time in tension

Of course, what we must not gloss over is the fact that there is a tension here: God is working with eternity as a framework. As we are often told: 'With God, one day is the same as a thousand years, and a thousand years is the same as one day.'[79] Which is rather frustrating for those of us who live in time!

A frustration expressively penned by one of the psalmists when he wrote: 'Wake up! Do something, Lord! Why are you sleeping!?'[80]

How many of us have been there?

Douglas Coupland, one of my favourite writers, says, 'Human beings are the only creatures who suffer time.'

Though in theory time is a constant, experientially it fluctuates, as any child knows who has waited for Christmas Day. The wait feels like an eternity, but the day itself flies by in what seems like an instant. A strange phenomenon that Albert Einstein bore witness to when he famously quipped: 'Sit on a hot poker for a minute and it seems like an hour. Sit a pretty girl on your lap for an hour and it seems like a minute.'

But these are frivolous examples. The reality for many people is that suffering time can be a test of endurance – physically, emotionally and spiritually. Though we all live in hope that our pain and longings are short-lived, we also have to face up to the fact that the unique peculiarities of time have the potential to make any wait seem unbearable.

Of course, being outside the vagaries of time, God doesn't have to suffer time in this way, but . . . 'When the time had fully come, God sent his Son.'[81] In Jesus, time and eternity meet. The God who is outside of time becomes a human being restricted by it.

Again, this is another reason why it's so important that we don't forget the humanness of Jesus.

Of course, for some, the arrival of Jesus meant the realization of patient waiting. His mother, Mary, for example, has not only waited patiently, as all expectant mothers do, but she also recognizes that here in Jesus the fulfilment of an ancient promise is upon Israel.[82] Zechariah, too, senses a long-waited-for liberation and peace,[83] while Simeon and Anna see in Jesus hope for all peoples everywhere.[84]

None of this, however, meant that the tension of time and eternity had been lifted by Jesus' arrival. Indeed, in some ways it was reinforced. If, like Mary and Zechariah, you've been waiting for freedom and liberation from oppressors all your life, or if you're poor and politically and spirituality marginalized, then you're probably hoping that this 'Saviour' is going to bring about a revolution that's swift and total. You're going to be impatient for change.

How infuriating it must have been, therefore, to have witnessed a Saviour who chose teaching and service, suffering and sacrifice, rather than a quick rebellion. How Jesus must have tested the patience of his followers when he said things like: 'Mother, my time hasn't yet come! You must tell me what to do.'[85] Jesus is supposed to be the coming Saviour of the world, and he's asking his mum for advice! Did I miss something?

Jesus' ministry was not an instant solution to the problems of life.

And neither is faith in Jesus today going to bring about an instant resolution to the tensions and sufferings of a life lived in time.

Of course, sometimes miracles do happen in an instant. But that's not the thrust of what the biblical narrative teaches. Miracles are one-off moments, an in-breaking sign of something that has yet to be. A future that is coming, but has yet to fully materialize. There is a patient God at work in the miracles – and a Spirit-led, patient people who occasionally encounter them. But miracles are not the norm. That's why we label them 'miraculous'. They are out of the ordinary and beyond the mundane.

Normal, even for Jesus, is the patient wait.

The act of waiting

I asked a friend: 'What value is there in patience?'

Her answer: 'It's what you do with the wait that's important.'

I guess I have a tendency to think of patience as something inactive. A waiting around for things to change, for life to become what it currently isn't. Certainly, when I was younger I felt like I was . . . sitting around . . . killing time . . . twiddling my thumbs . . . living a stopgap life. I wasn't a patient person – and in many ways I'm still not. But I am beginning to learn the value of patience.

I like the idea that what we do with the wait is the most important thing – that waiting is the opportunity to do something positive and become a better person for it; to reflect on life; to consider life's options; to pray (and wait for an answer); to build hope; to develop faith; to refine our character; to connect with people and build relationships; to serve others, and to gain wisdom.

One of the most valued commodities in Scripture is wisdom. Yet it cannot come in an instant. Even Jesus had to allow himself the time to grow wisdom.[86] Wisdom is gained in the long patient wait, through joyful experience and long suffering. It's the fruit of a considered life, not a blinkered rush. Yet in many Western cultures, youth is valued, not age. We fill our lives with advertising slogans, celebrity sound-bites and bubblegum lyrics, not long-won wisdom.

Our impatience is a poverty.

Of all the Fruit of the Spirit, patience fits the metaphor most appropriately. It is suggestive of the wait, the maturing, the allowing to ripen and become what would be impossible without this process.

I guess life's a little bit like watching *Dr Who* as a kid. The gap between the cliff-hanger and the resolution gives us time to contemplate and consider, to think about what we should do. The patient wait allows us to mature a little, to become wiser and more rounded – and with the Spirit's help, more Christ-like – as we patiently wait for God to resolve what he has started.

Jesus once told a parable about patience: 'The Prodigal Son'.[87]

Not that we always read it as a parable of patience. For most it is a parable about God's forgiveness. We see a celebrating father, running down the road to greet his son, throwing his arms around him, delirious with joy as he smothers him in kisses. But such uninhibited celebration belies the pain of waiting that the father must have gone through.

What we miss, perhaps due to the brevity of the story, is that this is a long-lost son. How many days did that same father stand on that roadside, straining his gaze into the distance, trying to conjure his son from the desert sands? How many distant silhouettes raised his hopes, only to turn out to be passing strangers or simply mirages, invoked by a combination of heat and a broken heart?

What we need to see when we read this parable is that the road the father ran down to greet his son was one of his own making, worn by his tireless patience as each day, he waited.

Of course, we may well ask: Why didn't the father leave his home, go in search of his son and physically bring him home, or at the very least try to reason with him? The truth is, sometimes a parent knows that however strong their will, a child's can be stronger, and so all they can really do is patiently wait for them to return home.

Being patient can seem like a lonely endeavour, but it is also a Godly one.

With patience, we can find ourselves.

With patience, God waits for us to come home.

A Kindness Revival

'Join Me!'

With these two simple words, the comedian and broadcaster Danny Wallace created a cult of kindness with thousands of devotees. Not that he always had so many followers. As Danny says of himself: 'I am not a man who was born to lead. I am a man who was born to stay in bed and have cups of tea brought to me at hourly intervals!'

But, for reasons I won't go into here, back in 2002 Danny decided to place an advert in a London newspaper which simply read: 'JOIN ME.'

All people had to do to join Danny was send him a passport photo of themselves to prove they were serious.

To this day, Danny can't understand why people responded. Was it simply out of intrigue? A sense of fun or adventure, perhaps? Or a fundamental need to belong? Whatever the reasons, respond they did – in their thousands.

The problem for a man who likes to stay in bed was that his followers soon became restless, demanding to know what their mysterious leader required of them. What had they joined by sending him their photo? Given that Danny couldn't bring himself to tell them that they'd joined nothing in particular and this was simply the result of a pointless whim, he came up with a single and simple purpose for the Join Me devotees: to carry out 'Random Acts of Kindness'. He even created a name for his followers, 'The Karma Army', and decided that these random acts should take place on Fridays, which were now designated 'Good Fridays'. And, just so his followers knew he was serious, Danny asked them to sign a newly drafted 'Good Friday's Agreement'.

Now, every Friday, the Karma Army take to the streets, wherever they live, and bring kindness into the lives of complete strangers. Not great big gestures, but small, yet significant moments of generosity. Carrying shopping for people. Paying for cups of tea. Handing out boxes of chocolate in the street. Delivering flowers to care homes. Leaving cakes on people's doorsteps.

As Danny admits, not world-changing stuff. But certainly life-affirming. People being kind for no other reason than it's good to be kind to other people.

Which it is, isn't it?

As the website states, the Karma Army is non-religious and non-political. It's about walking into a pub, buying a pint, putting it on a stranger's table, and walking away. It's not about being thanked, or getting any credit, or going to heaven. It's not even about changing humanity. It is simply about being human.

The problem is, being kind isn't as straightforward as it sounds.

Contemporary Western society in particular has developed a very sensitive social etiquette when it comes to the invasion of personal space. What's more, for some reason, we've become really suspicious of people who want to be kind to us. We don't trust people, especially those who do something for nothing. And that fact undermines the simple human act of being kind to people.

As Danny himself has observed through this experience, 'Being nice has gone from being second nature, to being fifth or sixth. We don't go and help, because we're afraid of being seen as weird, or eccentric, or as a potential mugger. Instead, we walk off, and we simply forget about it.'

I'm not a member of Danny's Karma Army. But I was brought up, not dragged up. My parents instilled in me that kindness is an appropriate virtue to have as a human being. And yet, I understand Danny when he says society makes it difficult to be kind.

One Friday, I was in my local supermarket when I noticed an old gentleman who looked a little confused and distressed. It turned out he'd tried to buy his shopping with a credit card that had expired and didn't appear to have any other means of paying for his groceries. So, given that the supermarket is a business and not a charity, they'd taken his now packed shopping away and were systematically unpacking it in front of him and putting it back on the shelves, like he was some naughty schoolboy!

Here's what was on my mind: One day I'm going to be old and confused and turn up at the supermarket without the means to pay. What's more, how did any of us know whether this man had any food at home to eat?

So, I said to the woman tilling up my shopping, 'I'll pay for his groceries.'

Well, you'd have thought I was trying to hold up the supermarket by the look that came across her face. No, 'Oh, that's kind, sir,' or 'How generous! How would you like to pay?'

All I got was the Spanish Inquisition (which I didn't expect) as to why I would possibly want to do such a thing (obviously, 'a random act of kindness' wasn't an appropriate answer), as well as huffs and puffs of inconvenience because they had to re-pack all his stuff for him.

I have to say, I don't think all the kerfuffle helped the gentleman's confused state. But he eventually twigged what was going on and insisted he wanted to pay me back.

He never did.

But as Danny Wallace suggests: we don't do kindness because we are looking for reward or thanks, or to be paid back. We do it because it's about being human.

Oxymoron

I find the idea of setting up the Karma Army rather inspirational.

But I also find it rather saddening.

At one level, it's a story about how good human beings can be. It makes me feel all soft and warm inside and brings a smile to my face to think that every Friday, somewhere, someone is encountering a random act of kindness from a complete stranger. But on reflection, it is also a sad indictment on our society. Clearly, Danny's followers are happy to be kind, but it also suggests that until they bought into the idea of Good Fridays, they didn't feel it appropriate, or weren't inclined to actually act kindly, for whatever reason.

But what bothers me more is this: How have we ended up in a place where kindness has become something that stands out as a random act?

The very fact that you can even have acts of kindness that are random, haphazard and indiscriminate, suggests to me that there is little, if any expectation that we can live in a world where people are kind on a day-to-day basis, or that being kind is a perfectly normal and appropriate way to live your life.

Of all the Fruit of the Spirit, surely kindness is one of the most ordinary, human and humane. Therefore, it should be as pervasive as humanity itself. Kindness should be a norm that is at the heart of who we are and so at the heart of our communities. There shouldn't be the need for Good Fridays, or isolated moments when kindness breaks into our world.

I agree with Danny – people are basically good. But goodness is no use to anyone unless it manifests and expresses itself in action.

But now I'm jumping ahead of myself. Goodness will have to wait until later.

For me, 'random kindness' is an oxymoron. They are two words that don't go together.

As I've already said, to call ourselves human is to recognize our spirituality and bring to mind that we are creatures called to reflect the image of the One who created us. Which means that kindness must be central to who we are, both in terms of our individuality as persons, and within our relatedness as family, community and society – not a bolt-on extra that occasionally and randomly appears.

But here is something that is random.

I settle down at my desk to write this chapter, opening up the relevant document to begin work, when out of the corner of my eye I catch that I've got mail. Given that I'm prone to procrastination and easily distracted from my task, I click open my email account. It's the Monday morning 'Word for the Week' from my friends over at LICC (the London Institute for Contemporary Christianity) – and the word they've got for me is this: 'Kindness'.

Actually, according to Margaret Killingwray, who wrote the aforementioned reflection, the word (in Hebrew) is actually *hesed*, 'loving-kindness'. Of which God says:

> *Don't boast about your wisdom, or strength, or wealth. If you feel you must boast, then have enough sense to boast about worshipping me, the Lord. What I like best is showing kindness* [hesed], *justice and mercy to everyone on earth.*[88]

But not only is kindness intended to reach everyone, whoever, or wherever they are, there's no sense that God only does kindness on Fridays as a random act. Every day is designated a *hesed* day because, 'The Lord's kindness never fails. . . . The Lord can always be trusted to show *hesed* each morning.'[89]

But this isn't a 'let go and let God' moment: Great, God is being kind to everyone today, so I don't have to be.

We are living, walking, talking icons of the invisible God. We are multi-dimensional icons, as opposed to two-dimensional ones painted on wood. Therefore, we are called to be active participants within God's creation. As such, God demands that we too designate every day a *hesed* day.

God has told us and shown us what is right: 'See that justice is done, let mercy be your first concern, and walk humbly with your God.'[90]

Dot to dot

The writer and activist, Jim Wallis, passed through my hometown while I was writing this book, so I took the opportunity to go and hear what he had to say for himself.

It turned out that what the man was preaching was revival. But not, as Jim says, the type of revival that 'Gets people into the Church and stops them having sex.' What he was preaching was a 'Justice Revival'. Or to put it another way: not the type of revival that says, 'I want you to get up out of your seats and come down to the front', but the sort of revival that starts with the words, 'The Spirit of the Lord is on me . . . to preach good news to the poor.'[91]

Sorry, I'm jumping around here, trying to join up some dots.

I agree, we need justice revivals. More than that, I think God would have us preach justice revivals in line with Jesus' message of Good News. But God also wants *hesed* to permeate life, because justice and mercy flow out of an attitude of loving-kindness towards the world.

Injustice, in all its forms (economic, social, political and religious), exists in our world for all kinds of reasons. But I want to suggest boldly that injustice persists in our world for one reason only: because there is a poverty of kindness.

At the end of the day, it might turn out to be a case of chicken versus the egg. But if we are going to see a revival of justice, then we are also going to need to preach a Kindness Revival.

Local kindness

I think it was Woody Allen who said that 'Ninety per cent of humanity simply show up.'

That's a little unkind. But I do think the majority of us could do a whole lot more than we actually do when it comes to living lives of kindness.

To defend humanity further from the wit of Woody Allen, I guess it's all too easy to get overwhelmed by the amount of kindness that's needed in the world around us. Turn on the news most days of the week, and anyone with an ounce of compassion or empathy is likely to be numbed by the deluge of horror, suffering, injustice, conflict, poverty, sorrow, loss, death and destruction that seems to happen on a daily basis.

Faced with wall-to-wall need, we become overwhelmed, and freeze. What kindness we have to offer is put on hold. We tell ourselves that our kindness wouldn't really make any difference. It would merely be a drop in the ocean. . .

But, isn't the ocean made up of drops?

Kindness is a collective: It's your kindness + my kindness + your neighbour's kindness + our church's kindness + our community's kindness + our society's kindness + God's kindness.

But your drop of kindness *is* needed.

There's no tick-box option on your birth certificate that reads: 'Do you wish to simply show up? ☐'

But don't be too hard on yourself. If you feel compassion, then you're halfway there. You've engaged your emotion. You've felt the pangs of empathy. You've become aware of need, and you at least know the desire to do something, even if you don't know quite what to do. Liberation theologians call this *conscientization*.

And you're not on your own in this process of seeing and feeling. More than one of the Gospel writers records that 'Jesus saw . . . and had compassion.'[92] And in the book of Exodus God tells Moses that he has '*seen* how my people are suffering . . . and I have *heard* them beg for help . . . I *feel* sorry for them, and I have come down to rescue them.'[93]

Daniel Goleman puts it like this: 'To feel with, stirs the act for.'

Therefore, if you can't act globally, then, as the saying goes: Think globally, *act* locally.

Let's face it, Jesus came with the intention of being the Saviour of the world. You can't get more globally minded than that. But, given the restrictions of his biological make-up, and the fact that there weren't any budget airlines or cable TV, Jesus was left to act out his kindness in the towns and villages of a provincial backwater of the Roman Empire.

The Saviour of the world broke bread and gave it to the hungry.[94]

The Saviour of the world ate with those no one else would eat with.[95]

The Saviour of the world tended the sick.[96]

> The Saviour of the world listened to those no one else wanted to listen to.[97]

> The Saviour of the world prayed for its people.[98]

> The Saviour of the world was aware of the global problem, but he saw and responded at a local level, contributing drops of human kindness, to which he added the invitation, 'Come, follow me.'[99]

The reality is, through television, radio and digital media, the majority of us know what's happening on the other side of the world. We are far less likely to know the need on our doorstep. Yet, it is this local need for kindness on which we can have the most significant impact.

There are no miracles required here. No challenges beyond the ability of mere mortals to respond. Just simple acts of kindness, compassion, empathy and care, such as giving out food to the homeless, or even offering them shelter on a winter's night. Visiting the housebound to see if they need any shopping doing. Volunteering to help with literacy skills in a local school. Having a cup of tea and a chat with someone who is lonely or mourning a loss. Cooking a meal for a single parent who is struggling to cope. Looking after the kids of a single parent so they can go out, or simply have a rest! Cleaning or gardening for someone who is ill or infirm. . .

Local life is a continuous opportunity to act kindly.

Global kindness

Having said all the above, I think the advent of digital media, the interconnectedness of the world economy, and the concept of the global village raise profound questions as to what it actually means to think globally and act locally. The shrinking world of the third millennium adds fresh pertinence to that most ancient of questions: Who are my neighbours?[100]

I feel privileged to be part of the Live Aid generation, which exploited the upcoming communication technology to feed the famine-stricken country of Ethiopia and shame politicians, world leaders and giant corporates into doing something about the injustices of this world – the same generation that gave us Jubilee 2000, Make Poverty History and the Millennium Goals.

Ultimately, however, all this new media and global-village mentality merely serves to amplify the agenda of that most archaic of communication technologies – a book. For when we read the Bible, or listen to it being read, it is not simply God's Word that we hear. We also hear the voices of those who need our kindness: the orphan and the widow, the oppressed and the marginalized, the poor and the sick.

And these are not simply distant voices trapped within an ancient text. They are as contemporary and present as the next sunrise. They transcend the stories in which they live and become voices for the voiceless in our world: the enslaved and the dispossessed, the refugee and the abused, the imprisoned and the dying, the old and the infirm, those who mourn and suffer, the starving.

Though Danny Wallace and his Karma Army might have stolen the thunder when it comes to generating initiatives that call on people to do random acts of kindness, the Church of England's *Love Life, Live Lent* campaign, which runs on a similar principle, does serve to challenge the Christian community by recalling the words of an ancient prophet and reminding us that the true fast is to give, not to give up:

> *I'll tell you what it really means to worship the Lord.*
> *Remove the chains of prisoners who are chained*

unjustly.
Free those who are abused!
Share your food with everyone who is hungry.
Share your home with the poor and homeless.
Give clothes to those in need; don't turn away your
relatives. [101]

Catching kindness

However you work out your human kindness, whether at a local or a global level, always keep this in mind: one of the beauties of kindness is that it is contagious.

By simply eating with Zacchaeus, Jesus transformed his life. What was seen as an act of undeserved kindness caused another, with Zacchaeus giving money to the poor and repaying what he had stolen. You could say, he was converted by kindness and converted to kindness. [102]

I too have known the kindness of strangers, as have my family. People who barely knew us, supported us through what would have otherwise been testing times. And, due to that undeserved kindness, I now feel indebted. Not to those individuals, for they wouldn't want that. Rather, I feel indebted to the universal kindness of humanity, created in the image of a kind and loving God. So I try and act kindly, dropping my offering into the ocean, hopefully causing some ripples that spread beyond my small world.

Who knows? My simple (even random) acts of kindness might just start a kindness revival.

A PERMANENT BECOMING / Seven
Good, for Goodness' Sake

> *God looked at the light and saw that it was* good. . . .
> *God looked at what he had done and saw that it was* good. . . .
> *God looked at what he had done, and it was* good. . . .
> *God looked at what he had done, and it was* good. . . .
> *God looked at what he had done, and it was* good. . . .
> *God looked at what he had done, and it was* good. . . .
> *God looked at what he had done. All of it was very* good. . . .[103]

In the beginning, God created a *good* world. And most people were happy that this was the case until, a few billion years after the event (or a few thousand, if you're that way inclined), an influential theologian called Augustine managed to convince most of Christendom that God had in fact created a world that was 'perfect' – an idea that has largely persisted in Western Christianity ever since.

Of course, on paper this looks a sensible conclusion to make. God, if he is worthy of such a name, would surely be perfect. Therefore, to create a universe that was anything less than a reflection of God's own perfect nature would seem a rather peculiar thing to do. So, God must have made it perfect, just like he is.

The problem is, ideas about perfect worlds probably come from Platonic philosophy rather than the Bible. In reality, there's very little, if any evidence to suggest that God intended to create a world that was perfect. Certainly, the opening chapter of Genesis never asserts that this was God's intention. That's why early church leaders, such as Irenaeus, decided they were going to stick with what has to be the more obvious reading of what the Bible says: that God created a world that was *good*. An idea that is carried into the present day by Eastern Orthodox Christianity.

Naturally, we need to be careful what we try to derive from a story that relies on symbolism, metaphor and wordplay in order to reveal its purposes and truth. Narratives, like the one found in the first couple of chapters of Genesis, are notoriously difficult to interpret.

Theological consensus is going to be a vain hope, and anyone claiming to make propositional statements from what is, after all, a creation 'story', should be avoided like the plague.

That said, the bigger story derived from ideas about a good creation, over and above a perfect one, has a certain appeal and makes a lot of sense.

A good plot

God created a *good* world for one very simple reason: *good is better than perfect*.

A perfect world has nowhere to go. It is static, fully formed, finished and complete. Which seems rather unbecoming of a creative, loving, relational God.

A good world, on the other hand, has the potential to grow more goodness. Good is dynamic, creative, fruitful and purposeful. Which sounds more like the God we read about in the Bible.

What's more, God made human beings in his image. A likeness that wasn't perfect, and therefore static, but a *good* likeness that was also intended to be dynamic, creative, fruitful and purposeful, after God. We were created good so as to join God in bringing about more goodness in the world.[104] So, rather than perfection, there is ongoing creation: good begetting good.

However, God's ultimate intention for his good creation is this: that we all come to reflect *the* archetypal Person – Christ Jesus. Or as one of the New Testament writers puts it, 'God's purpose is that we become mature, attaining the whole measure of the fullness of Christ.'[105]

And the fact that humanity was created good, rather than perfect, allowed for that purposeful and creative maturing to take place.

Of course, we don't normally think about the story in this way. But it's important that we do, because it gives both Christ and ourselves our intended place in the overarching plot. Goodness gives Christ and ourselves a place, purpose and relationship independent of that other overarching story: the redemption of the world from sin.

God planned for us to do good things and to live as he has always wanted us to live. That's why he sent Christ to make us what we are.[106]

A good plot gone bad

The problem with all this talk about a creation that's established good in order to bring about more goodness is that there is, at times, such an obvious lack of goodness in the world. Terrible things happen of such inexplicable magnitude that the only word we can find to describe them is 'evil'.

Classically, the first human beings are said to have made rather a mess of things by deliberately and wilfully disobeying God's explicit imperative not to eat from the tree that would provide them with the knowledge of good and evil.[107] Eating the fruit caused humanity to 'fall' from perfection, taking everything else in creation with them.

Which is rather unfortunate for those of us who came after the event.

The problem is, it's hard to see how evil can get a foothold into a world that's perfect. Surely, perfection precludes the possibility that even the slightest trace of badness or evil could have raised its head in God's paradise. As the Christian writer Schleiermacher once pointed out, 'Evil must have come from somewhere, but if God created the world (including human beings) perfect, there should be no way for it to go wrong.'

Ironically, a good world also sorts out the problem of how evil gets into the creation. As we've said, a good creation has the potential to produce more goodness. But it's also open to the possibility that it will fail to continue in that process and so atrophy, becoming stunted or immature, or worse still, deny its good origins altogether, producing badness and evil.

Unfortunately, this idea that God intended good for humanity and the creation is what the serpent undermines in the mind of Eve.[108] You see, underlying Adam and Eve's disobedience in regard of God's request not to eat from a particular tree was a far more primitive and basic issue than simple pride or rebellion. They doubted God's goodness.

God *had* created a good world – but was it good enough?

And with this doubt, and its subsequent actions, Adam and Eve interrupted the maturing process that God had set in motion. In other words, there was no 'fall' from perfection. Rather, there was an overreaching to become something human beings are not – God – which resulted in a failure to embrace God's intention for them: to bring goodness to the world and so become fully mature, authentic human beings after Christ.

Not so much a paradise lost, but paradise unattained.

But this process wasn't confined to the Garden of Eden. We mustn't let the words 'In the beginning . . .' make us think that these problems have passed, or that somehow we are not part of this story. As my friend Brian McLaren says, 'This is the story we find ourselves in.'

And the purpose of the story is to help us orientate our own lives, to help us see that we too doubt God's good intentions for us and the creation. What's more, this lack of trust leads to either a prideful rebellion against God, and an attempt to become something we are not (which often results in actions that can be described as evil), or far more commonly, we simply fail to realize our full potential as human beings and to join God in bringing goodness to the world.

Both these realities are what the Bible calls 'sin'.

Residue

Did you know that the universe resonates with the remains of the Big Bang?

If you have access to a radio telescope, you can listen in to its underlying hum.

Did you know the creation also resonates with the goodness of its good origin?

Whatever state the world is in, however far away it is from the original intentions God had for it, he hasn't ceased to declare it good – it has a residue of goodness.

Of course, sometimes it's hard to see and hear that residue. This good world has become stained and polluted by sin. There is suffering, evil, war, terrorism, murder, child abuse, famine, genocide, corruption, sickness and disaster. It seems delusional to say this is a good world.

But it is a good world.

We must not let ourselves become so obsessed with sin that we obliterate the goodness we find in the world. We mustn't allow the media and politicians to over-paint the goodness with fears of terrorism, and the spinning of crime-statistics for political gain. When our leaders draw a line on an inanimate map and declare it to be an 'axis of evil', we must tell ourselves that the majority of the people who live in that area are as good as anyone who lives in the so-called 'civilized world'.

Even in the darkest moments of human history – the holocaust, the killing-fields of Cambodia, the genocides of Rwanda, or the terror of 9/11 – miracles may have been rare, but human goodness wasn't lacking. People still cared for one another. People tended to the suffering of their fellow human beings. People even sacrificed their lives to save others.

This is a good world flecked by evil, not an evil world where goodness occasionally breaks in.

Think of it this way: Imagine the number of opportunities people around the world today might have to commit an antisocial act, from rape or murder to simple rudeness and dishonesty. Make that number the bottom fraction. Now for the top value, put the number of such antisocial acts that will *actually* occur today. . . . That ratio of potential to enacted meanness holds as close to zero any day of the year. And if for the top value you put the number of benevolent acts performed in a given day, the ratio of kindness to cruelty will always be positive.

Though it takes a little thinking through, this illustration from Daniel Goleman is simply the raw statistic that the sum total of goodness vastly outweighs suffering or evil. The majority of people in this world still reflect the goodness of creation, despite the obvious presence of sin and suffering.

As John Steinbeck once wrote: 'Despite all our horrors and our faults, somewhere within us there is a shining.'

I, for one, need to hear this, as most of my Christian life I've been told that people are utterly depraved and lacking in any goodness at all. Which I found hard to square with the reality that every day I saw good people doing good things.

Of course, for some people, saying such things sounds like you're ignorant and avoiding what the Bible teaches. After all, 'there is no-one who does good'.[109] Not only that, but Jesus says that only God is good[110] (except Barnabas, apparently).[111]

The fact is, I don't think that Jesus is suggesting that people are devoid of goodness and utterly depraved. I think what he is saying is this: 'Remember the story you find yourself in – goodness starts with God. Don't call me good, as if I've got an ontology (a being) of goodness independent of God. If I'm good and do good things, then it's because of the fact that I'm connected to God through the Holy Spirit.'

Actually, wherever or in whoever goodness is found, its origin is always God. Therefore, goodness is theocentric, not anthropocentric. It comes from God, not from people. God is the perennial spring, and goodness flows into the lives of people through that one true source.

In any case, if we are honest, most people we know aren't openly rebellious when it comes to God, or determined to do evil rather than good. They're probably a bit lost, life-questioning, soul-searching, generally good, but not quite feeling good enough. They're unsatisfied, there's-something-missing kind of people.

Which is actually what the Bible says people are like, most of the time.

To summarize an observation by the theologian Mark Biddle, when the Bible talks about humanity's sin, it more often than not uses the idea of falling short, or missing the mark (in Hebrew, *ht'*; in Greek, *hamart*). That is, a biblical view of humanity is to assume that people want to hit the target, to be what God wants them to be, to be good, to be fully human, to be Christ-like. The problem is, we fail to hit the target. We are like archers who aren't very good at archery.

So, Paul writes in his letter to the Romans that every human being fails to live as God intends: 'For we all sin and fall short of the glory of God.'[112] In doing so, Paul isn't suggesting that every human being is depraved, rebellious and evil. What he is saying is that every human being fails in some way to live the life God intended.

Bumper stickers

One of the most perplexing questions of theology and philosophy is why there is so much evil and suffering in a world created by a good God.

Any theory that tries to give an answer to this question is called a theodicy.

A theodicy can be a complex, pedantic and at times awkward weaving together of philosophical and theological arguments to try and wrestle with and understand why, for example, people are cut down in their prime with cancer. Or why people leave for work or school and never come home. Or why people would want to fly a plane into a skyscraper, killing thousands of innocent people. Or why tens of thousands of people are wiped out in an instant by a tsunami. Or why a child would want to gun down another child in cold blood. And why God doesn't do anything to stop all this.

Some theodicies are complex. Others more simple.

'Teacher, why was this man born blind? Was it because he or his parents sinned?'[113]

This is a theodicy at work in the minds of Jesus' disciples. People are sick or suffer because they've done something wrong. Job's friends argued out of the same worldview to try and explain suffering, basically saying: Job, you must have done something wrong for God to allow you to suffer so much.[114]

God rebuked Job's friends for such warped thinking,[115] and neither will Jesus entertain such nonsense from his disciples.[116] There's no room for this sort of blame game when it comes to people's suffering.

Which is why it astounds me that such thinking is surprisingly prevalent among Christians in the twenty-first century. I've heard 'Christians' argue that a person is terminally ill because they've got unrepented sin in their life. I've heard 'Christians' suggest that people died in the tsunami that hit Asia in 2006 because they didn't worship the 'Christian' God. Or simply because developers 'sinned' by building ramshackle housing in low-lying areas.

How did we become so twisted?

I can't claim to have a fully worked-out theodicy. Perhaps God's response to Job might suggest that such things are beyond human understanding.[117] Which causes me to think that perhaps it's not our place to build a theodicy for ourselves, but rather to simply acknowledge the meaninglessness of some suffering; to face up to the reality that life is not wall-to-wall goodness; to place alongside our 'Smile, Jesus Loves You' car stickers, the most famous bumper sticker in the world: 'S**T HAPPENS!'

The reality is, in this world inexplicable and meaningless suffering happens. And to acknowledge and accept this leaves us not with the question, 'Why?', but with an altogether more positive question: 'How should I respond?'

For to allow suffering to take place without a good response, or to face evil without demonstrating that goodness still exists, and that ultimately goodness will prevail, removes the only grounds for hope that people may have when facing life's tragedies.

The return of goodness

I know I've used this analogy before, but it bears repeating once again in this context: Creation is bringing forth something good out of chaos.[118] And in creating human beings in his image, God placed within us that same mandate – to bring goodness out of chaos. Just as God created through the Spirit in the beginning, so God breathes into individuals and into his community, the Church, so that we may also become a creative, life-giving, life-affirming, chaos-denying force within a creation that knows tragedy and suffering.

We are to be agents of transformation that have been transformed ourselves by the presence of God's Holy Spirit in our lives. Or as someone else put it, 'We are God's workmanship created in Christ Jesus to do good works, which God prepared in advance for us to do.'[119] Not a specific, pre-ordained shopping-list of things peculiar to us, but a more general call to seek opportunity to do good where the presence of God's goodness is needed; to follow the example of Jesus, who, led by the Holy Spirit, went around doing good.[120]

Just in case you've missed it: Doing good is an essential of the gospel, the good news!

Bringing goodness to the world isn't an optional extra.

There's no room for the attitude: 'I've got a faith that gets me to heaven, where everything will be good, so that's OK.' Likewise, repenting of your sin isn't simply dumping all the bad stuff you've done at the foot of the cross and walking unburdened into heaven when you die. Repentance isn't just the decision to stop doing non-good; it's also, and perhaps more importantly, the determination to pro-actively *follow* Jesus by seeking to do good, with the help of God's Spirit. After all, faith that doesn't lead us to do good . . . is dead![121]

Can't you just hear the taunts: 'A do-gooder! Who wants to be a do-gooder?'

But doesn't that bring us back to where we started? In the Garden of Eden the serpent's trick was to make doing the wrong thing more attractive than doing the right thing: 'Oh Eve, who wants to be a do-gooder?'

Post-Eden, our trick is to make goodness more attractive than the alternative. It's to make goodness so appealing that people are drawn back to the source of all true goodness, and so forward into the fullness of creation and maturity as human beings made in the image of a good God.

So, let's not become weary of doing good,[122] but instead, let's encourage one another to bring goodness to the world.[123]

Faithfulness that Falters

> *'Faithless is he that says farewell when the road darkens,'* said Gimli.
>
> *'Maybe,'* said Elrond, *'but let him not vow to walk in the dark, who has not seen the nightfall.'*

I've never read Tolkien's *The Fellowship of the Ring* (and I probably never will), but I love this quote. My friend Holger pinned it to my bedroom door while we were still students. I then placed it in a small wooden box that I keep for mementoes, and it's still there some ten years later. It was the first thing that came to mind when I began thinking about this chapter, for Gimli and Elrond's little exchange pretty much encompasses the elements of what true faithfulness is:

Faithfulness is born out of relationship.
Faithfulness cannot be called faithfulness unless it is tested.
Faithfulness is not a one-off promise, but a continuous, determined, ongoing re-commitment to love, trust, believe or follow.

In many ways, it reminds me of the story of Ruth in the Old Testament.

Ruth's faithfulness is born out of relationship with her mother-in-law, Naomi. But it's a faithfulness that's tested when both women find themselves widowed. Naomi decides to return to Israel, encouraging Ruth to go back to her own people, fearful that she will be poor and unmarried for the rest of her life if she insists on remaining faithful to her adopted family. Ruth, however, becomes a paradigm for a faithfulness that is continuous, determined and ongoing. Her intent is captured in these words:

> *Please don't tell me to leave you and return home! I will go where you go, I will live where you live; your people will be my people, your God will be my God. I will die where you die and be buried beside you.*[124]

Of course, the story of Ruth is one with a happy ending.[125] Something that can't be said for every story of faithfulness. In that sense, while much can be taken from it, it's not necessarily a typical story of the fruits of faithfulness. Some may even suggest that on balance, it's atypical. Certainly, I've known friends who have shown faithfulness no less committed than Ruth's (both to other people and to God), but have been left bereft and questioning what purpose is served by being faithful.

I think honesty would have to say, there are no easy answers to offer.

That said, I still think faithfulness should be something we value and are determined to pursue, even if there is no guarantee of a return on our investment. Indeed, perhaps true faithfulness lies in that telling phrase, 'as yet' – though, clearly, it's a moot point whether our impatient culture likes the sound of that, or values a faithfulness that has true longevity built into its meaning. After all, our own relationships can so often be fleeting and open; marriages continue to collapse with frightening ease; and career-chasers step over friends and colleagues, or move from company to company, in search of better salaries and more perks and power.

But that's not to make a move to single people out. I think it's fair to say that few of us find faithfulness without reservation or qualification easy. From politicians who make commitments in manifestos to get our votes, only to fail to deliver once they are in power, to the more mundane and empty promise of 'I'll call you', we're frightened of being faithful just in case we think something better will come along. As a result, we live in a world of cheap commitments where words come easy and actions can wait until I can work out the benefits to me.

Which begs the question: Does anyone really care about being faithful to anyone any more – except to one's self, that is?

Maybe I'm being overly pessimistic and cynical. Perhaps what's really going on is that, like goodness, a residue of faithfulness still pervades our culture – or at least the desire to be faithful does. Perhaps most people aren't wilfully unfaithful, and in reality our intentions are, more often than not, to remain faithful to promises and commitments made in good faith. Be they the personal, one-to-one words, 'I will love you always', or a political promise made to an entire nation, such things start as a genuine, heartfelt desire to remain faithful. The problem is, such faithfulness so easily falls by the wayside when the going gets tough, or life's circumstances change. That's why any commitment to be faithful needs to be continually revisited and re-invested with meaning as life's rollercoaster peaks and troughs.

Faithful to . . .

As with all these virtues, to speak of faithfulness is ultimately to speak of something that has its origins with God, and which manifests itself in our lives as a Fruit of the Spirit. But in saying this, we are also constantly reminded that such virtues are not simply born out of our connection to God, but are developed and deepened by human relationship. So, faithfulness isn't something that simply 'exists' in us; rather, it is grown in the soil of interrelatedness between the Spirit of God and human community.

The fact is, faithfulness cannot be grown by preaching it from a pulpit, nor can it be gained by reading about it in the pages of a book. Faithfulness is something that has to be nurtured. It has to be worked out in a specific context. It has to be given opportunity to become an actuality of people's lives, rather than simply words without action. Faithfulness has to be an achievable reality, rather than a nice idea that's merely seen as idealistic.

All this becomes obvious when we read the narrative of the Gospels. Jesus didn't simply preach from hillsides or pulpits, or suggest people go and read stories of the great people of faith and assume that this was sufficient to generate faithfulness in his audience. Instead, Jesus lived out the purpose of incarnation to its fullest, placing himself in relationship and community. He gathered friends and followers in order that faithfulness might have a context and a reference point, and so that it might be modelled, tested and continually proven through lives that shared the experience of trials, as well as triumphs.[126]

Though some may baulk at the suggestion, in certain ways, I even think Jesus placed himself in relationships with others in order to grow his own faithfulness. Certainly, he felt the need to have friends with him when his own faithfulness was tested concerning his impending death on the cross, which he had already indicated he was willing to face – but that's not the same as actually doing so! So, in the Garden of Gethsemane, he appealed to Peter, James and John, his closest friends: 'Stay here and keep awake with me.'[127]

When I read these words, I hear such fragility and humanness in Jesus' voice – 'Stay. Don't let me face this darkness alone. Help me be faithful.'

Of course, there is more than one dimension to this story, and we shall return to it later.

A few years ago, some friends asked me to say a few words at their son's dedication. At such an important event in a young person's life, there are all kinds of things one could say. But what came to my mind as I reflected on this privilege was this: at a dedication, the community is being entrusted with the development of a child. We are not only being asked to support the parents; we are actually being addressed, as individuals and as a community, to commit to being faithful in our responsibility to nurture this new life.

I guess the same is true of a marriage ceremony. Yes, the couple commit to faithfulness in their wedding vows, but the community is also being asked to engender a context that encourages and enables that faithfulness to grow, to see out the struggles of life and avoid unnecessary challenges that might threaten to undermine that commitment.

God recognizes and affirms this communal and relational dimension of the development of faithfulness when he places the baby Jesus into the midst of a community and into the arms of Mary and Joseph.[128] Long before he takes up his ministry as an adult, nurturing the faithfulness of others, Jesus is entrusted as a vulnerable baby to a community who are called to be faithful in seeing that he develops and grows. Obviously, to suggest that Jesus' faithfulness was fully nurtured in the small rural community of his childhood would be conjecture. But equally, it would be harsh in the extreme to suggest that having someone with the faithfulness of Mary as his mother had no impact at all on Jesus.

In all this, a simple point is being made: faithfulness grows out of and within faithful relationships and faithful communities. Faithfulness is a Fruit of the Spirit, which is modelled and learned and imbibed in human relatedness.

That's why it's vital that communities of faith are communities of faithfulness.

That's why it's vital that from the earliest possible opportunity, the children of our communities see, hear and witness faithfulness taking place within healthy human relationships – because much of our culture will try to instil in them the counter-narrative that at best, faithfulness is a self-serving virtue, if it has any benefit at all.

To coin an advertising slogan, which pretty much sums up many people's attitudes to faithfulness, if your current commitments don't suit, then 'simply switch'. That there's nothing to gain from faithfulness is a very potent and very real message of contemporary life.

I really think we need to hear the words of the faith-development specialist, Ivy Beckwith, when she writes that:

> *Spiritual formation . . . is never about how many programmes a church has, or even about the quality of those programmes. It is about the attitudes and quality of the people the children interact with and the overall spiritual and relational quality of the community of faith.*

Though we rightly place a strong emphasis on telling, teaching and preaching the biblical narrative within our faith communities, in reality, children will dismiss all of this unless they see genuine, authentic people living out those stories of faith and faithfulness. The fact is, for better or for worse, children will be impacted more by the people of God than by the story of God. Therefore, we need to live out a genuine, authentic mutuality within our communities, and have relationships that are open, honest, trustworthy and faithful. For such things stay with a developing and growing child into adulthood.

Testing times

Like all aspects of human life closely linked to relationships, there are good times and there are bad times when it comes to faithfulness. Few, if any, of us are fully faithful in our relationships with each other and our relationship with God. Not, as we've already suggested, because we desire to be deliberately unfaithful, but rather because faithfulness, particularly over the course of many years or a whole lifetime, is a frustratingly difficult thing to achieve.

Therefore, to have relationships and communities that are honest, open, trusting and authentic, we need to accept and acknowledge the fact that faithfulness often falters. Indeed, adopting an attitude of acceptance may well lead to greater faithfulness, ironic and paradoxical as this may seem.

What's more, it will bring ourselves and our faith communities closer to the ebb and flow of faithfulness that is openly accepted within the biblical narrative. For on the pages of the Bible, there is a to-ing and fro-ing between faithfulness and unfaithfulness that is the norm, even if it isn't the ideal.

From Abraham, through the Old Testament stories of exodus and exile, to the disciples of Jesus, we read of faithfulness that falters. Which brings us back once more to the events surrounding the Garden of Gethsemane – a place where even Jesus' faithfulness is tested.[129]

On their way to the garden, Jesus suggests to all the disciples that they will reject him – something they all vehemently deny will ever happen, claiming that they will remain faithful even if it means they have to die with him.[130] Of course, some of the disciples have made such promises before.[131] But that was with the comforting presence of their mother by their side, not in the reality of the encroaching darkness of the cross. The disciples are promising to be faithful while they still have Jesus very much alive and present. They're committing to faithfulness from within a certain comfort zone, or in the belief that Jesus has got all this talk about impending death wrong. They're saying they will be faithful even unto death, because they don't believe they will have to be.

What was it that Elrond said? 'Let him not vow to walk in the dark, who has not seen the nightfall.'

And the night does fall, and the promised faithfulness of the disciples does falter, if only temporarily.[132]

Of course, such faltering shouldn't surprise us, given the exceptional circumstances surrounding the crucifixion. But some words of Jesus spoken from the cross point us to something that is seldom discussed, even though it's very much part of the biblical narrative:

it's not just the faithfulness of ordinary people which comes into question, but the faithfulness of God himself.

Where's God gone?

The Old Testament theologian, Walter Brueggemann, suggests that God's people have in their metanarrative (the big story) two elements, which are held in tension. Firstly, there is the God who creates, who makes promises and covenants with his people, who leads them out of slavery and delivers them from exile, who performs miracles and is very present. This story Brueggemann calls *Israel's Core Testimony*. But Israel also have a *Counter Testimony*, a story in which God appears not only distant, but actually absent. What's more, vast swathes of the story of God's people contain this apparently absent God, causing the prophet Isaiah to lament: 'Truly, you are a God who hides himself.'[133]

Of course, the place to really find God's apparent absence, and doubts about his faithfulness, is within the writings, liturgies, poems and songs of the psalmists:

> *How much longer, Lord, will you forget about me?*
> *Will it be forever? How long will you hide?*[134]

> *Why are you far away, Lord?*
> *Why do you hide yourself when I am in trouble?*[135]

> *Wake up! Do something, Lord!*
> *We are flat on the ground, holding on to the dust.*
> *Do something! Help us!*[136]

> *Our Lord, where is the love you have always shown*
> *And that you promised so faithfully to David?*[137]

> *My God, my God, why have you deserted me?*[138]

These final words we quite naturally associate with Jesus as he utters them while dying on the cross. They tell us that he too experienced the counter testimony of a God who sometimes appears to hide and abandon us at the most inopportune moments.[139]

But in being quick to read this psalm as something prophetic that foresees the cross, we fail to read it in its simplest form, as the existential reality, the actual experience of the original psalmist – an ordinary person who no longer senses the presence of God. Which is a shame, because it's as a psalm that it is more able to resonate with our own experience of faith.

Saint John of the Cross, the sixteenth-century mystic, coined the term, 'the dark night of the soul' as a way of expressing this same absence and questioning of God's faithfulness. For even though Christians are blessed to live in post-resurrection times, Christ has not yet come again. God is not fully present with us. We live with the 'already' of the cross and resurrection, but dwell in the 'not yet' of the full completion of the new creation. The tension between the core testimony and the counter testimony still applies.

At any given moment, for every Christian who can claim blessings and the closeness of God, or give witness to answered prayer, or even a miracle, there are many Christians who long for an answer, who are begging God to come close. Who know that 'My God, why have you forsaken me?' is still a valid and all-too-common question to ask.

Of course, if God were tangible, or if easily identifiable signs of his existence confronted us everywhere, we would all live in the fullest light and with unshakeable faithfulness. But so often, we look for God and, like the psalmist, discover that he is not there. We doubt God's faithfulness, even as we hold onto the legitimate expectation for God to do something and prove that he is faithful – for after slavery came freedom, and after exile came return, and after the cross came resurrection.

But such stories simply serve to re-emphasize the fact that real faithfulness is the kind that keeps walking into the darkness; that faithfulness isn't governed by the experience of Easter Sunday, when everything appears OK, and we can breathe a sigh of relief, but by the emptiness and blackness of Easter Saturday, when all traces of God appear to have gone from the earth.

As my own wife has taught me, the truest form of faithfulness is to be found nestling among the crippling agonies of doubt and the dark night of the soul.

And on . . .

As I was writing this book, Brian Kolodiejchuk was publishing a series of private letters, written by Mother Teresa, which in collected form he had entitled, *Come Be My Light*. They were being touted as a startling revelation and insight into contradiction and dissonance. For what they revealed was that Mother Teresa had lived the last thirty years of her life within the counter testimony. She had done the vast bulk of her service to the poor with no sense whatsoever of the presence of God – yet she had remained faithful to God and to her work.

On one occasion she wrote to her friend and spiritual confidant, Revd Michael van der Peet, 'The silence and the emptiness is so great that I look and do not see, listen and do not hear.'

Here was one of the great contemporary icons of faith, whose work was so totally and publicly connected to her faith in God, privately suffering the torment of the dark night of the soul.

It's a story that perfectly encapsulates the fact that faithfulness is not a one-off promise, but a continuous, determined, ongoing recommitment to love, trust, believe and follow – sometimes on a day-to-day basis, and sometimes without response from the one you are being faithful to. Therefore, her letters aren't an insight into contradiction and dissonance, but a testimony of faithfulness that was sustained by the poor she served and the friends she confided in.

I'm married to someone who more often than not hears nothing but the silence of God. At times, Kay has suffered utter turmoil and crippling doubts that God even exists, or worse still, that God exists but that he doesn't care. Yet she has remained faithful to this God who is absent, partly because, like Mother Teresa, she has allowed other people to carry her through the darkest moment.

Reflecting on this battle between doubt and faithfulness, Kay once wrote that all relationships entail courage and risk. So, we need to continually and courageously walk the path of faith and take a risk with God, for if he is who he says he is, then ultimately he will prove faithful.

The Power in Gentleness

'MEEK. MILD. AS IF.'

I saw these words one Easter. They were written large underneath a stylized picture of Jesus outside a church. The poster's designers had taken the famous image of the Marxist revolutionary, Che Guevara (which adorned the walls of many a student room in the 1960s and 1970s), and simply replaced his beret with a crown of thorns and . . .

Voilà – Jesus the Revolutionary.

I guess the purpose was to make Jesus appear more edgy, enigmatic, iconic, tough, street-wise and appealing.

The whole effect was topped off with an invitation: 'Discover the real Jesus. Church.'

Which kind of placed a rather heavy burden on congregations up and down the country. I mean, people might have actually turned up at church after seeing this poster and discovered that the only revolution going on was the replacement of instant coffee with an espresso machine.

Caffé latte, anyone?

Of course, this image of Che Guevara is one of the best-known graphic portraits of the twentieth century. Perhaps only Andy Warhol's screenprints of Marilyn Monroe and Elvis (and, ironically, Guevara) would be more easily recognized by the general public. So on paper, I'm sure the advertising gurus thought this was a great idea. After all, we're a culture driven by symbols and sound-bites.

What you've got here is a clever double-take: an image of Guevara that becomes Jesus, right before your eyes.

You've also got a great sound-bite – 'Meek. Mild. As if.' – that works as a counterpoint to the popular conception of Jesus as someone who liked nothing better than gathering little children around him to tell them sweet stories about his Daddy in the sky.

Much as I like the poster, not least because it's a relief from the amateurish attempts you usually see on church notice-boards, I think it's fundamentally flawed.

First of all, it links Jesus to the kind of revolution that is the antithesis of his own life and the means by which the kingdom of God is established. While I'd be the first to agree that Jesus' intention was revolution, he wasn't a revolutionary in the same way as Guevara, who was involved in violent overthrow.

What's more, questioning the 'meekness' and 'mildness' of Jesus alongside this image not only serves to associate him further with aggressive revolutionary ideals, but it suggests that there is something inherently wrong with such human attributes.

To me, it implies that meekness and mildness are unappealing and have less value than . . . well, to be honest, I'm not sure what's being inferred. Should I be reading the poster with antonyms in mind?

'BRUTAL. ANTAGONISTIC. THAT'S MORE LIKE IT!'

Is this just one of those attempts to 'sex up' Jesus for our contemporary world?

Do we need to mess around with our images and ideas about Jesus because we don't know what to do with the real Jesus?

Do we misunderstand and misread him, and so become embarrassed to suggest that the way of Jesus can be culturally relevant and cutting-edge?

After all, 'gentle Jesus, meek and mild' doesn't sound like he's going to be much use in the cut and thrust of life in the twenty-first century.

What the world needs is Jason Bourne and Jack Bauer, not Jesus Christ.

Part of the problem we face is that our Christian bookstores are full of Christian schmaltz: twee trinkets that associate Jesus' truly revolutionary teaching with pictures of puppies, and saccharine-sweet poems that we've dared to call 'inspirational'. We've allowed Jesus to become sentimental and soft. Which then makes it virtually impossible to meaningfully and purposefully use words like 'meek' and 'mild' (and related words, such as 'kind', 'good' and 'gentle'), because we've built up a context of fluff, and an interpretive framework of chintz, through which we are forced to read such words. In doing so, we've robbed ourselves of a biblical Jesus who would allow us to understand them completely differently.

All of which has ramifications for us when seeking to value and build a contemporary Christian faith around the Fruit of the Spirit. After all, half of these virtues share a similar semantic domain as the words 'meek' and 'mild'. Which means we're not a million miles away from disparaging the very things that make us Christ-like.

'KIND. GOOD. GENTLE. AS IF.'

What we need is a paradigm shift in our understanding and appreciation of such virtues, so that our faith communities can take part in Jesus' revolutionary intent, establishing the kingdom of God through kindness, goodness and gentleness, and so allow the world to see the value and power of such virtues.

Throughout the biblical narrative, gentleness and power are held in tension, paradoxically equated with each other, and juxtaposed. Even in the opening lines of the Bible, the power needed to create the universe, and suppress the chaos of those first few moments, is predicated to the comparatively gentle actions of breathing and speaking,[140] rather than some divine brute force, physical exertion, or even a cosmic battle (an idea present in the neighbouring Babylonian creation story).

That God chooses to manifest his power gently is picked up again in the story of Elijah.

It starts with Elijah duly recognizing God as 'The Lord God All-Powerful'.[141]

But how is this all-powerful God revealed?

> *All at once, a strong wind shook the mountain and shattered rocks. But the Lord was not in the wind. Next, there was an earthquake, but the Lord was not in the earthquake. Then there was a fire, but the Lord was not in the fire. Finally, there was a gentle breeze, and when Elijah heard it, he covered his face with his coat. He went out and stood at the entrance of the cave.*[142]

Clearly, such creative actions and divine encounters aren't intended to play down God's power. Truth be known, they are emphasizing it.

In the case of the creation story, it could well be forming part of a polemic against other stories about gods who claim to have created the universe. It's as if God is saying, 'Look at all the fuss and bother, posturing and violence that's involved in such claims. I have so much power in reserve, to breathe is enough for me to create life.'

As for God's encounter with Elijah – well, thunder-bolts and lightning might be what's expected of the gods, but such obvious demonstrations of power are usually a sign of an inferiority complex. God is, who God is (I am, who I am); therefore, it's unnecessary for him to strut around. Indeed, God prefers to be present in a reserved and gentle manner wherever possible, for this more meaningfully and purposefully reflects the God who is love.

The truth is, only the truly powerful are free to act gently in the way God does.

True gentleness, which originates from God, is power under control and reserved strength. God is the archetypal gentle giant. He is like a father, gently cradling his new-born child in his arms, seemingly without effort – yet within those arms is more than enough power to do real harm. Or to change the metaphor: God's gentleness can be equated with that of a lioness, who carries her cubs in the same jaw that she will use to crush the life out of a wildebeest in order to feed them.

It's within such a framework that we are to understand the idea of a gentle Jesus. For when we encounter Jesus in the narrative of the Gospels, we come face to face with someone who had the power and the resources to crush his enemies in a moment. He could overthrow empires, eradicate corrupt political and religious systems, and lay waste idols and temples of gods who set themselves against the God of Israel. But he wasn't that kind of a revolutionary.

Compared with the power at his disposal, Jesus touched the world and people's lives rather gently. Sure, he got angry at times, most famously when he cleared the temple of the money-changers.[143] But this is always strength under control. It's doing what is sufficient, and what's appropriate in order to further the kingdom of God, and to achieve God's purposes.

It's not a gentleness that lacks power. Rather, it's a way of being in the world that has the ability to bring about revolutionary change, through relatively gentle means, in situations that would have most revolutionaries reaching for their swords and raising rebel armies, not gathering women and children on hillsides to teach them: 'Bless you, meek and gentle people, you will inherit the earth.'[144]

Of course, in the Zealots, the people of first-century Palestine had revolutionaries in the style of Guevara, willing to strike violent and rebellious blows against their Roman occupiers. In the celebratory songs of Mary and Zechariah at the beginning of Luke's Gospel, there are suggestions that the expectation of the people was for a Saviour who might just lead them in a battle to overthrow their enemies.[145] Even John the Baptist goes on to tell the people, 'Someone more powerful is going to come.'[146]

What a context for Jesus to finally bring his message! What is he going to say? What is he going to do?

> *Jesus returned to Galilee with the power of the Spirit. . . .*
> *he went to the meeting place on the Sabbath . . . and*
> *read, 'The Lord's Spirit has come to me, because he has*
> *chosen me to tell the good news to the poor. The Lord*
> *has sent me to announce freedom for prisoners, to give*
> *sight to the blind, to free everyone who suffers, and to*
> *say, "This is the year the Lord has chosen."'*[147]

What we so often fail to realize when we read these verses, is that as far as the people are concerned, Jesus has forgotten something. Everyone in the room would have been holding their breath, waiting for Jesus to finish. They knew what was coming – revolution and overthrow was in the air. Here comes what they've been waiting for! People are on the edge of their seats, when suddenly . . .

Jesus stops reading and sits back down.

The ending people are expecting is conspicuous by its absence.

'Where,' everyone is asking, 'is the promise of revolution? Doesn't Jesus know that this passage in Isaiah ends, "This is the year when the Lord God will show kindness to us *and punish our enemies*"?'[148]

Of course he does.

But Jesus isn't interested in their agendas, nor in quoting Isaiah word for word. Rather, Jesus is painting the picture of *his* revolution – a revolution not without its power, but one that wields authority through a gentle Spirit, not through violent and brutal overthrow and revenge. He knows what the people desire, but it will be on his and God's terms, and not by employing divine power in the way so many earthly individuals and corrupt systems would like to. What the people must learn is that the Old Testament prophets Zechariah and Isaiah saw how things would be:

> *Everyone in Jerusalem celebrate and shout! Your king has won a victory, and he is coming to you. He is gentle and rides on a donkey.*[149]

> *I will give him my Spirit, and he will bring justice to the nations. He won't shout or yell or call out in the streets. He won't break off a bent reed or put out a dying flame, but he will make sure justice is done.*[150]

Perhaps men need to hear this connection between power and gentleness more than most. With increasing talk about the feminization of the church and the recent glut of sentimental 'Jesus is my girlfriend'-type worship songs, I know many men who are questioning what they've got themselves into. They want to follow Jesus, and be a disciple, but they're unsure of the picture being painted. While men are happy to see gentleness in their mothers and wives, they're not so keen to be associated with it. For within women, men can see that gentleness is a virtue, but within themselves, and set against our culture's perception of what it is to be a man, it is merely perceived as a sign of weakness.

But the point is (as with so many things), Jesus repaints gentleness and its relationship to power and strength. It's a central vision of the kingdom of God that the strong should carry the weak. But the weak need carrying *gently*, and only the truly strong are capable of such an action.

Given the world in which we find ourselves, we must accept that there is a need for powerful responses to poverty, injustice, terrorism, violence and oppression. But we also need to realize that the Fruit of the Spirit, such as kindness, goodness and gentleness, are not the antitheses of power, but are the strength with which we are to work against the world's problems and bring about God's kingdom.

Tread gently

When I think about power and its relationship to gentleness, I can't help but turn my thoughts to the way human beings are ravaging God's creation. From global warming to the exploitation of natural resources, humanity is flexing its muscle and demonstrating its power, but we are hardly exercising it gently.

We may not feel that powerful in ourselves as individuals, but as a collective, humanity's power is massive, and currently we are treading far too heavily on what is a fragile earth.

At the moment, there are 6 billion people living on this planet.

In a few decades' time, there will be at least 9 billion.

As the title of Al Gore's documentary states, it's 'an inconvenient truth' that unless we change our way of being in the world, the earth simply won't be able to sustain that many people living the way we do.

Of course, thanks to people like Al Gore, and movements such as Greenpeace and Friends of the Earth, we are waking up to the fact that our lifestyles need to change, and our exploitation needs to stop. Indeed, the increasing desire of many to reduce their carbon footprint is a great metaphor for a growing vision that living lives of gentleness has the power to make a genuine difference.

But there's more to 'treading gently' than just our carbon footprints.

Currently, there are 1 billion people on the planet who don't have access to a clean, safe and accessible water supply. Which means that millions of people die each year from drinking dirty water. Many children (especially girls) don't receive an education because they are needed to fetch water for their families, and women cannot work to contribute to the economy of the home because they too spend hours every day walking to find water.

The United Nations says 20 litres per day is the minimum human need for water. Yet many people in developing countries are forced to survive on just 5 litres – the amount you and I use in flushing the toilet.

But what really makes our water footprint so heavy is our consumption of 'virtual water' – that is, the water needed to produce the consumables that we so love.

A jar of coffee needs 20,000 litres (or 20 tonnes) of water to produce it. It takes around 25 baths full of water to produce enough cotton for that T-shirt you're wearing. Rice needs up to 5,000 litres of water to produce 1 kilo – and so the list goes on. . . .

Each of us consumes thousands of litres of virtual water a year in what we buy – and most of it is being drawn from water supplies in some of the most water-stressed and poorest countries on the planet. As the writer and campaigner Fred Pearce has commented in his book, *When the Rivers Run Dry*:

> *The water 'footprint' of Western countries on the rest of the world deserves to become a serious issue. Whenever you buy a T-shirt made of Pakistan cotton, eat Thai rice or drink coffee from Central America, you are influencing the hydrology of those regions – taking a share of the River Indus, the Mekong or the Costa Rican rains. You may be helping rivers run dry.*

Of course, there are all kinds of complex economic, international trade and development issues tied up in this comment, but the fact is, there are ways of re-shaping economics and wealth-creation, and yet, without water, there will be no people in these countries with whom to trade.

Paul wrote to the Philippians: 'Let your gentleness be evident to all.'[151]

I'm reliably informed that 'gentleness' here could be translated 'humaneness':

'Let your humaneness be evident to all.'

In the face of global warming, the world water crisis, and other environmental and humanitarian crises, our humaneness needs to be evident in the gentleness with which we touch this earth that God has given to us.

In this, the twenty-first century since he first spoke them, perhaps Jesus' words, 'Blessed are the meek and the gentle, for they shall inherit the earth', become less of a promise and more of an imperative.

Ecce Homo
Back in 2003, I published the book *The Lost Message of Jesus* with my then boss, Steve Chalke. By way of an epilogue, Steve drafted some personal thoughts, which he simply entitled, 'The Scandal'. He conjured with images of Mark Wallinger's life-size sculpture of Jesus, *Ecce Homo* ('behold the man'), which was installed on the vacant plinth in Trafalgar Square to mark the Millennium. Being life-size, 'Jesus' was dwarfed by the other memorials of leaders and generals, which are all over-blown, massively scaled-up representations of their real-life counterparts.

Actually, there were two sculptures of Jesus in Trafalgar Square that Millennium New Year.

Perhaps rather fittingly, only a few metres away from Wallinger's effort was another life-size representation of Jesus that few visitors knew about – a newborn Jesus, nestled among some straw, which was part of the nativity commissioned by St Martin's in the Field, the church that lies on the edge of the square.

One crisp winter's night, I stood in front of this baby Jesus and crouched down.

There, in my field of vision, were the first and the final moments of Jesus' earthly life. Both figures of Jesus looked ordinary, human and helpless. A far cry from the overbearing images of power, politics and war that stood about them. To use Steve's description, 'Jesus looked inconsequential'.

One man who saw *Ecce Homo* was quoted as saying, 'You couldn't put your faith in someone like that; he's as weak as a kitten.' While one the UK's leading Christian publications commented: 'It looks so vulnerable, an anomaly, naked, a statue of weakness. Will it send out all the wrong signals?'

Which brings us full circle: 'Meek. Mild. As if.'

A Jesus of ordinary humanness – who was meek and mild, kind, good and gentle – appears to concern us. Such a Jesus feels like an embarrassing irrelevance in a world of global terror and impending environmental catastrophe.

And with such comments we state our ignorance, demonstrate our misunderstanding, show our lack of creative imagination, and prove the poverty of our apocalyptic and eschatological vision:

> *Look! The Lion from the tribe of Judah is the Lamb standing in the centre of the throne.*[152]

Ultimate power, strength beyond any earthly creature, is situated within, and employed by, a gentle Lamb.

Here, the writer of the book of Revelation is utilizing the same technique of double-take used by the advertising executives who designed the Jesus/Guevara poster – except this double-take works. The author has understood the relationship between power and gentleness, and portrayed it in a visual form without any sense of shame or embarrassment:

'JESUS. GENTLE LAMB. YES HE IS!'

'Self' Control

I think, therefore, I am.

Well, at least that's what René Descartes thought. Not surprisingly for a philosopher, his own thoughts had been on his mind for a little while before he made this famous statement. Thoughts, he thought, obviously exist, and because I think those thoughts, I must exist. Everything else Descartes thought about himself and the world, he pretty much doubted. Which makes him come across as someone who was a bit wrapped up in himself. No wonder one of my friends once retorted: 'Don't you think "I think, therefore, I am" is a poor summary of what it means to be human?'

Surely, we are far more than just a load of electrical impulses running around our heads?

Naturally, the obvious answer to that question is: of course we are. But, as Descartes' musings prove, 'Who am I?' is a question without a clear or straightforward response. For while you can understand what he might be driving at, I'm not sure many of us would be happy to summarize our existence by simply saying: 'I think, therefore, I am.'

Me, Myspace and iPod

It's fairly safe to say that a big part of our lives is taken up with the search for our true self, or the journey to discover who we are. And while tapping into the essential-me has been an obsession of people for a long time, over the last century or so, particularly in Western society, this has pretty much become the central preoccupation of most people.

Actually, rather ironically, you could argue that what *collectively* defines Western society is the fact that the majority of us are rampant individualists – that is, while we might have connections to family, friends, communities, clubs and other social groups, our first concern is the well-being, happiness, discovery and development of 'me'. What do I want from life? What career should I opt for? What relationships should I cultivate? What benefit will they have for me? Where should I choose to live? What should I do with my spare time? Who do I want to be?

What's more, our culture positively encourages us to become self-centred and self-obsessed. How many of us have had friends say things like: 'If it feels good to you, then do it.' 'If it's true for you, then that's all that matters.' 'What's important is that you be yourself. Be true to who you are.' As Richard Koch and Chris Smith said in their book, *Suicide of the West*: 'Never in human history has it been easier – indeed, almost mandatory – to do one's own thing.'

Individualism is at the heart of our culture, and at the heart of individualism is the idea that I don't need other people in order to be myself. I look into myself to discover me, and this inner-self I project outwards to the world – take it, or leave it.

Alongside our individualism (and probably as a way of reinforcing it), we have also become isolationists. Not that we entirely cut ourselves off from other people and become hermits. It's more that we cocoon ourselves (particularly via technology) from those immediately in our presence, preferring the sounds of our mp3 players and the silence of text messaging to actual conversation. This cocooning of oneself by technology has been described as 'urban trance'. We ignore people who share our immediate space, such as those tilling up our shopping, or the person sitting next to us on the commuter train, engaging instead with the 'world' created by our iPods and mobile phones. We also frequent online chat rooms and share our selves through email, blogs, Myspace, Youtube and Facebook. Over 9 million of us even have a virtual self (an avatar) frequenting the cyber world, 'Second Life'.

It would seem that at the very least, Descartes' ditty needs updating to: *I think – I text, I blog, iPod, I Myspace, I Facebook, I Second Life – therefore I am*.

Of course, one could argue that all this is building community and relationship by utilizing twenty-first-century technology. But in reality, it simply extends our ability to have such things on our terms and for the benefit of my self. What looks like greater connectedness, openness, accessibility, and inclusiveness is in fact largely controlled by me, and totally at the mercy of my whims. I manage the technology through which we relate. I can simply ignore you, edit you, and even delete you, if I so wish. I can start and end a relationship with you, and never have to leave the comfort of my armchair. 'I no longer care for your virtual self, so please don't invade Myspace.'

But to paraphrase my friend: Don't you think *'I think – I text, I blog, iPod, I Myspace, I Facebook, I Second Life – therefore I am'* is *still* a poor summary of what it means to be human? After all, as Norman Nie, Director of the Stamford Institute for the Quantitative Study of Society, once wrote: 'You can do an awful lot of things on the net, but you can't look someone in the eye, you can't shake their hand and you certainly can't give them a hug and a kiss.'

The point being made by Nie is that while such technologies can connect us, they are also limited, detached and can even be dehumanizing if they dominate our 'social' interaction. Our self needs more to develop and flourish than the occasional 'I luv u. x.' arriving in our Inbox. However autonomous, self-determining and isolationist we want to be, as human beings we need actual, physical, social interaction with others in order to thrive and discover who we truly are.

The exponential growth in communication technology, which means we can work anywhere we choose to, is coinciding with the most geographically and socially mobile population Western society has ever known. There are more people than ever before living on their own, either by choice, or by circumstance. Tight-knit communities and close family ties are being replaced by social dispersion, isolation and loneliness. Yes, a philosophy of individualism and liberty has brought our society, and ourselves, many positive things, such as human rights and personal wealth. But it has also brought us a culture that has a soaring victim mentality, high rates of depression and suicide, a strong sense of alienation, narcissistic tendencies, selfishness, lack of purpose, envy and greed.

Which begs the question, will Jesus be able to find words of comfort for such a society? After all, what are we giving him to work with?

> When you were lonely, I emailed you. When you suffered inner anguish, I texted you. When you were in need, I wrote on your Facebook wall. When you cried out for help, I was listening to my iPod. . . . Whenever you visited the Facebook profile of any of my people, it was the least you could have done.

Archbishop Desmond Tutu once contrasted Descartes' 'I think, therefore, I am' with an African saying: 'I am because you are; you are because we are. A person is a person through other people.' He went on to say this:

> None of us come into the world fully formed. We would not know how to think, or walk, or speak, or behave as human beings unless we learned it from other human beings.... the solitary, isolated human being is a contradiction in terms.

Archbishop Tutu's words point us to a great irony: our search for the self through autonomous, self-determining individualism has instead, more than likely, caused us to lose our selves. Starting with 'I' in isolation can never lead us to discover an answer to our preoccupying question, 'Who am I?' We need other people in our lives in order to become who we were created to be – which is obvious when you look at the God who gives us life.

'I' can't dance

It's one of the fundamentals of the Christian view of humanity that we are made in the image of God. And it's one of the foundational beliefs of the Christian faith that God is Trinity – three distinct Persons, who share the one essence: God (the Father), God (the Son), God (the Holy Spirit).

In order to try to explain this idea of God as Trinity, about three centuries after the resurrection, some church leaders came up with a metaphor: *perichoresis.* Which at first glance doesn't look like it's going to be that helpful. But all it really means is that God the Father, God the Son, and God the Holy Spirit form a divine dance, which requires coordination and mutuality. It's a dance that can't be danced without the interpersonal relationship found within the Trinity. But, at the same time, the form the dance takes allows the self-expression of each divine Person, enabled and supported by the others.

Of course, when I was a boy growing up within my local Christian community, nobody spoke of this *perichoresis.* The ministers and Bible study leaders didn't even speak about God being a dance, probably due to the fact that they, and their theology, were under the influence of a culture of individualism, and the search for the self – though I didn't think that way as a boy! Even faith in the twentieth century had become self-centred. It was about me and my God: 'I think (and understand), therefore, I am saved.'

Not surprisingly, theologies that buy into a philosophy of individualism generate metaphors that are self-centred and self-referencing. So, instead of starting with God (three Persons in a divine communion) and figuring out that in order for us to reflect

God, we too must be in communion with God and other people, we worked the other way around: '*I* am made in the image of God. Therefore, *I* must be three-in-one. How can that be? Oh yes! *I* am body, mind and spirit.'

The problem is, 'I am body, mind and spirit' is a fundamentally flawed description of what it means to be a person, and a totally unsuitable metaphor for understanding the Trinity. It buys into the idea that I don't need anyone else, not only to be me, but to reflect the God in whose image I am made. Which is quite clearly nonsensical. God is three Persons with one essence. Body, mind and spirit is three elements in one person. That's just one person, totally wrapped up in one's self – *me-myself-and-I*. Which isn't Christian theology, it's Cartesian philosophy – that is, thinking thoughts after Descartes, not after Trinitarian revelation.

As for linking it with the metaphor of a dance – well, such self-centred thinking is simply shuffling backwards and forwards, with my handbag in front of me, saying, 'This is my dancing space, don't invade it.' Which hardly reflects the kind of dance envisaged by *perichoresis*.

The truth is, when God said, 'Now we will make humans, and they will be like us,'[153] God was inviting us to join in the creative, fluid, mutual, life-affirming, relational dance of the Trinity. God didn't make us to be wallflowers, sitting on the edge of the dance-floor, looking on, timid and shy, wanting to take part but fearing to be asked. And God certainly didn't create us to find our own little spot and do our own thing with a handbag in front of us, protecting our own little corner of the dance-floor. Such dancing places our selves at the centre of our lives and acts like a centrifuge, ultimately pushing people away. By way of contrast, the dance in step with the Trinitarian God is centripetal – it draws people in by making space for them.

The reality that we are made in the image of a Trinitarian God should serve to pull us away from autonomous individualism into interrelatedness. It keeps at the forefront of our minds the truth that God is both personal and interpersonal – that is, relational. And, given that we derive our personhood from God, then we too must seek to live in such a way that affirms our self as an interpersonal human being.

We, Jesus

At the heart of the Christian faith stands the person of Jesus. But that's not the same as saying that at the heart of the Christian faith stands an individual. Clearly, Jesus' relationship to the Holy Spirit (already mentioned earlier in the book), and the idea of the Trinity as a dance, ensure that Jesus can never be viewed as an autonomous individual with an itinerant ministry. Indeed, Jesus is very keen that those who follow him understand that who he is, is inseparable from his relationship with God the Father and God the Holy Spirit. For Jesus is both one with the Father[154] and led by the Spirit.[155]

What's more, read the Gospels, and your are left in no doubt that Jesus knows who he is. Not only that, but he knows what life is about, and what his purpose and place is in this life. To put it in contemporary language: Jesus has discovered his true self. He has answered the question, 'Who am I?' Even better, Jesus even makes it clear how we too can find out who we truly are – which is pretty good news for twenty-first-century Westerners who are caught up in 'Project Me'.

The only problem is that Jesus' path to self-discovery is the antithesis of the route our culture so often takes:

> *You must forget about yourself. You must take up your cross each day and follow me. If you want to save your life, you will destroy it. But if you give up your life for me, you will find it.*[156]

Basically, Jesus is saying to us: 'If you want to find your self, look outward, not inward. If you want to discover who you are, go serve others. If you wish to learn to love yourself, then love other people. Ultimately, if you really want to know who you are, then know God.'

Suddenly, this isn't such good news. Giving up your life doesn't sound like a recipe of self-discovery. Actually, it sounds like a very risky business. Surely, it would make more sense to stick with 'Number One', to focus on me and my needs and desires and to love myself as a matter of priority, rather than controlling myself and putting others first. After all, self is safe. It keeps me in charge and leaves me to determine the course of my life. Losing-to-find doesn't sound such great wisdom.

I guess the question we need to be asking ourselves is this: Who do we trust?

Do we trust ourselves?

Do we trust the philosophy and the culture in which we live?

Do we trust the wisdom of the God who created us and determined what it means to be a person and a human being?

From the outset, God is clear: 'It's not good for a person to be alone.'[157] Whatever we tell ourselves, or allow our culture to tell us, the truth is, we can't become a God-intended person by being on our own. Ultimately, an autonomous individual cannot find or sustain his or her self. What's more, the further you take yourself away from relationship and into isolation, the less of a person you become. You may not feel this way. You may feel good about being on your own – for now at least. For as Jesus says, eternal life is to know God and to know Jesus.[158] Or put another way: Without God, without being in relationship, we cease to become and ultimately, we cease to be.

The reality is, only through God, in Jesus, via our relationship with the Holy Spirit, can we obtain and have life in all its fullness – now and always.[159]

Freedom to become

In many ways, the search for self is the search for freedom. Particularly in the West, the culture of individualism goes hand-in-hand with ideas of autonomy and self-determination, which have a ring of freedom about them. But is a life determined by 'I' really the kind of liberty that will allow us to become who we desire to be?

God knows that as human beings we prize our freedom – possibly above all other things. But God also knows that, above all other things, our becoming a Christ-like, God-intended person should be prized more. That's why, when the Bible says things like: 'Christ has set us free! This means we are really free',[160] or, 'Where the Spirit of the Lord is, there is freedom',[161] it adds commentary so that we can't misunderstand and assume God is authorizing our drive to greater autonomy, self-determination, isolation and self-centredness.

> *Don't use your freedom as an excuse to do anything you want. Use it as an opportunity to serve each other with love . . . love others as much as you love yourself.*[162]

Of course, we are not left on our own to try to love and serve others. A Christian spirituality can never be an autonomous, individualistic pursuit. Rather, the Holy Spirit works in us to establish *koinonia* – a fellowship of mutual, interpersonal, creative, life-affirming relationships.[163] As such, we become what Andrew Walker has described as 'an icon of the Holy Trinity'.

Not that our individual self, with its unique personality and gifting, is somehow going to be obliterated by the Holy Spirit, or that we are going to be absorbed into a homogeneous church, or become a Christian clone. For this would be counter to the image of God in which we are made. Freedom of expression, being who we are, is a Trinitarian outlook. For even though the Father, Son and Holy Spirit are one in purpose and intent, they have the freedom to express themselves as Persons with different personalities.

The truth is, in Christ, through the Spirit, we are free, truly free, but we are not independent. We have been set free to become our true self, to become a person: a Christ-like human being in relationship with other people and in relationship with an interpersonal, Trinitarian God.

A PERMANENT BECOMING / Epilogue

A Permanent Becoming

The poet, T.S. Eliot, once wrote:

> *We shall not cease from exploration,*
> *And the end of our exploring will be to arrive where we*
> *have started,*
> *And know the place for the first time.*

Though Eliot wrote these lines with something completely different in mind, I think they make an excellent summary of our permanent becoming as human beings towards a God-intended, Christ-like maturity. For, if we are to permanently become, then there can be no ceasing from an exploration of ourselves, the world in which we live, and the God in whom we believe. Emotionally, relationally, intellectually, culturally, creatively, imaginatively, theologically and, therefore, spiritually, there is always more to know, understand and deepen.

And yet, there is the very real temptation to think that we have arrived; to arrogantly believe that we know God, fully understand ourselves and others, and have an exhaustive grasp of what the Bible teaches (generally and specifically); and to feel that we have fully developed our insights and emotions. But if we are tempted to think this way, then we fool ourselves (or have been fooled by someone else), and have ceased to become – and that really is a human tragedy of biblical proportions.

I suggested at the beginning of this book that when God created us, he created us as human beings. And he wants to keep us that way. Whoever we are, whatever we're going to be, we are going to become that as a flesh-and-blood human being. Human is what we are and human is what we're going to stay. Therefore, despite the permanent becoming that is taking place in our lives through the work of the Holy Spirit, and the long journey towards Christ-likeness we are on, our exploration will end where it started – with ourselves.

But, here is the hope of the biblical narrative and the assurance of God: when we shed this mortal coil, and have it replaced with our imperishable natures, we will finally be what God intended us to be when he first envisioned our lives. And so, even though we will still be ourselves, we will know this 'place', this God-intended-me, for the first time.

I often say to people, in five, ten, or twenty years' time, I hope I'm not the same person as I am now. I hope my relationship with God has moved on, and that my understanding and beliefs will have been shaped, altered and improved by that relationship. If such things haven't happened, then I believe something will have gone fundamentally wrong. I will have become like the Adam of the creation narrative, stunted in my maturing.

The only way I know to prevent this occurring is to allow the Spirit of God to engender within me a permanent becoming towards a fully human, authentic Christ-likeness.

To that end, the Fruit of the Spirit is . . .

Love	**Joy**	**Peace**
Patience	**Kindness**	
	Goodness	
Faithfulness	**Gentleness**	
	Self-control	

Biblical References

Zero **Under the Skin**
1. Galatians 5:22–23.
2. 1 Corinthians 13:8.

One **Being Human – Becoming Like Jesus**
3. Acts 17:28.
4. Philippians 2:6–7.
5. Luke 3:22; 4:1, 14, 16–18.
6. Genesis 1:2.
7. John 6:63; 14:16–17; 16:13; etc.
8. Genesis 1:27; 2:7 (author's own paraphrase).
9. Matthew 5:3 (NIV).
10. Matthew 6:10.
11. 1 Peter 1:16.
12. Genesis 2:18.
13. John 13:34–35.
14. Matthew 22:39.
15. John 13:1–17.
16. 2 Peter 1:5.
17. Philippians 2:12–13.
18. Philippians 1:6.

Two **Love Is . . . As Love Does**
19. Galatians 5:22 (NIV.
20. 1 John 4:8.
21. 1 John 4:19.
22. Luke 6:32.
23. Exodus 20:2.
24. John 3:16; 1 John 4:9–10.
25. John 14:9.
26. John 15:13 (NIV).
27. 1 John 3:16.
28. Luke 4:16–19.

29. Luke 6:32, 35.
30. John 15:12.
31. 1 John 4:20.
32. Matthew 25:35–40.
33. Colossians 3:14.
34. John 1:9.

Three **The Joy in Happiness**

35. Luke 10:21.
36. Psalm 65:9–13.
37. Romans 8:22.
38. Revelation 21:4.
39. Isaiah 35:10.
40. Hebrews 12:2.
41. 1 Peter 1:8.
42. John 16:33.
43. Psalm 16.

Four **Peace, Imperfect Peace**

44. Ecclesiastes 3:1, 8.
45. Revelation 21.
46. Revelation 22:20.
47. Genesis 1:3.
48. Genesis 1:2.
49. Numbers 6:24.
50. Isaiah 32:15–20.
51. Isaiah 65:17–24.
52. Revelation 21:3–4.
53. Luke 2:14.
54. John 14:27.
55. Matthew 14:24–25; cf. Genesis 1:2.
56. Mark 4:39; cf. Genesis 1:2.
57. Matthew 9:6.

58. Matthew 15:33, 36–37.

59. John 15:5.

60. Luke 5:12–14.

61. Luke 14:15–24.

62. John 8:11 (author's own paraphrase).

63. John 11:25, 43–44.

64. Isaiah 1:15–17.

65. James 3:18.

66. Matthew 26:11.

67. Matthew 5:38–45.

68. Colossians 1:21–22.

69. Ephesians 2:14–18.

Five **The Patience of a Sinner**

70. Hebrews 13:8.

71. Revelation 1:8.

72. John 14:6.

73. Genesis 1:1.

74. Genesis 12:1–3.

75. Hebrews 11:39.

76. See the book of Exodus.

77. Malachi 3:1.

78. Revelation 21:5 (author's paraphrase).

79. 2 Peter 3:8.

80. Psalm 44:23.

81. Galatians 4:4.

82. Luke 1:55.

83. Luke 1:68–79.

84. Luke 2:22–38.

85. John 2:4.

86. Luke 2:52.

87. Luke 15:11–32.

Six A Kindness Revival

88. Jeremiah 9:23–24.
89. Lamentations 3:22–23.
90. Micah 6:8.
91. Luke 4:18.
92. Matthew 9:36; Mark 6:34.
93. Exodus 3:7–8.
94. Matthew 14:19.
95. Luke 19:7.
96. Luke 5:12–13.
97. John 4:9, 27.
98. John 17.
99. Matthew 9:9.
100. Luke 10:29.
101. Isaiah 58:6–7.
102. Luke 19:1–10.

Seven Good, for Goodness' Sake

103. Genesis 1:4, 10, 12, 18, 21, 25, 31.
104. Genesis 1:26–30; 2:15.
105. Ephesians 4:13.
106. Ephesians 2:10.
107. Genesis 2:17.
108. Genesis 3:1–5.
109. Romans 3:12 (NIV).
110. Mark 10:18.
111. Acts 11:24.
112. Romans 3:21.
113. John 9:2.
114. Read the first half of the book of Job for the full picture.
115. Job 42:7.
116. John 9:3.
117. Job 38 – 42.

118. Genesis 1:2–3.

119. Ephesians 2:8–9 (NIV).

120. Acts 10:38.

121. James 2:17.

122. Galatians 6:9 (NIV).

123. Hebrews 10:24 (paraphrase).

Eight Faithfulness that Falters

124. Ruth 1:16–17.

125. Ruth 4.

126. John 18:25–27; cf. John 21:15–19.

127. Mark 14:34.

128. Luke 1:26–38.

129. Matthew 26:36–46.

130. Matthew 26:31–35.

131. Matthew 20:20–22.

132. Matthew 26:40, 56, 69–75.

133. Isaiah 45:15.

134. Psalm 13:1–2.

135. Psalm 10:1.

136. Psalm 44:23–26.

137. Psalm 89:49.

138. Psalm 22.

139. Matthew 27:46.

Nine The Power in Gentleness

140. Genesis 1:1–3.

141. 1 Kings 19:10.

142. 1 Kings 19:11–13.

143. Matthew 21:12–17.

144. Matthew 5:5 (author's paraphrase).

145. Luke 1:46–55, 68–79.

146. Mark 1:7.

147. Luke 4:14–19.
148. Isaiah 61:2.
149. Zechariah 9:9–10; see also Matthew 21:5.
150. Matthew 12:20.
151. Philippians 4:5 (NIV).
152. Revelation 5:5–6.

Ten 'Self' Control

153. Genesis 1:26.
154. John 10:30.
155. See Luke 4:1.
156. Matthew 16:24–25.
157. Genesis 2:18 (author's paraphrase).
158. John 17:3.
159. John 10:10.
160. Galatians 5:1.
161. 2 Corinthians 3:17 (NIV).
162. Galatians 5:13–14.
163. Acts 2:43–47; 4:32–35.